A Guide to

C000175896

It is vital that coaches have the ability to recognise mental health problems in their clients, enabling them to make an informed decision about whether coaching is appropriate. *A Guide to Coaching and Mental Health* provides an indispensable introduction to the assessment of psychological issues in the context of coaching.

Divided into three sections, the book covers all the legal, ethical and practical considerations. Section 1, Working on the Boundary, starts by exploring the distinction between normal and abnormal behaviour. In Section 2, What's Being Said?, the authors introduce fictional case studies, which cover a range of possible mental health issues from mild depression and anxiety, through to psychoses and potentially life-threatening problems. Section 3, Categories of Mental Illness, guides the reader through the definition and management of the more common mental health problems.

This accessible and jargon-free guide to identifying mental illness will prove invaluable for coaches and other related professionals, whatever their level of experience.

Andrew Buckley has, for ten years, worked as an individual and team business coach and counsellor. He is a member of the training faculty of the William Glasser Institute and an accredited member of the British Association for Counselling and Psychotherapy.

Carole Buckley qualified as a doctor of medicine in 1980. She is passionate about holistic care, in particular encouraging the understanding of the relationship between mental wellbeing and social and professional functioning.

Essential Coaching Skills and Knowledge
Series Editors: Gladeana McMahon,
Stephen Palmer & Averil Leimon

The **Essential Coaching Skills and Knowledge** series provides an accessible and lively introduction to key areas in the developing field of coaching. Each title in the series is written by leading coaches with extensive experience and has a strong practical emphasis, including illustrative vignettes, summary boxes, exercises and activities. Assuming no prior knowledge, these books will appeal to professionals in business, management, human resources, psychology, counselling and psychotherapy, as well as students and tutors of coaching and coaching psychology.

Titles in the series

A Guide to Coaching and Mental Health
Andrew Buckley & Carole Buckley

Achieving Excellence in Your Coaching Practice
Gladeana McMahon, Stephen Palmer & Christine Wilding

Essential Business Coaching
Averil Leimon, Francois Moscovici & Gladeana McMahon

A Guide to Coaching and Mental Health

The recognition and management of psychological issues

Andrew Buckley and Carole Buckley

Routledge
Taylor & Francis Group

LONDON AND NEW YORK

First published 2006
by Routledge
2 Park Square, Milton Park, Abingdon, Oxon OX14 4RN

Simultaneously published in the USA and Canada
by Routledge
711 Third Avenue, New York, NY 10017, USA

Routledge is an imprint of the Taylor & Francis Group, an informa business

Copyright © 2006 Andrew Buckley & Carole Buckley

Typeset in New Century Schoolbook by
RefineCatch Limited, Bungay, Suffolk
Paperback cover design by Lisa Dynan

British Library Cataloguing-in-Publication Data
A catalogue record for this book is available from the British Library

Library of Congress Cataloging in Publication Data
Buckley, Andrew, 1958–
  A guide to coaching and mental health : the recognition and
management of psychological issues / Andrew Buckley & Carole Buckley.
     p. cm. – (Essential coaching skills and knowledge)
  Includes bibliographical references and index.
  ISBN 0-415-39458-9 (hbk) – ISBN 0-415-39459-7 (pbk) 1. Mental health
counseling. 2. Mental illness–Diagnosis. 3. Counseling. I. Buckley, Carole,
1955– II. Title. III. Series.
  RC466.B93 2006
  616.89'14–dc22

                    2006008645

ISBN 13: 978-0-415-39458-1 (hbk)
ISBN 13: 978-0-415-39459-8 (pbk)

ISBN 10: 0-415-39458-9 (hbk)
ISBN 10: 0-415-39459-7 (pbk)

ISSN 1749-1185

To Jane and Edward, without whose continual support and patience this book would not have been written. (AB)

To Mike, Jenny and David for their love, help and support. (CB)

Contents

SECTION 3
Categories of mental illness, their definition, epidemiology and management   **179**

List of figures and tables

Figures

Tables

Foreword

by Mike Nowers

It is a startling fact that one in every three or four patients attending a general practice surgery, or family doctor, will be suffering from some form of mental disorder. This may range from simple anxiety or emotional distress, through depression to severe but thankfully rare illnesses such as schizophrenia or mania. Mental illness affects all of us at some time either directly or through friends, family or work colleagues and is no respecter of gender, wealth or position!

What is also a sad but undeniable fact is that of all the illnesses that affect human's mental illness is the least understood and the most feared and ridiculed. It is no surprise that many people with mental illness pretend that it does not exist or hide their symptoms from family and friends rather than confess to suffering. This means that they may well be in the workplace, often in responsible or potentially dangerous circumstances when not at their best and prepared to deny, often vehemently, that there is anything wrong with them.

A further complication is that most mental illnesses lie on a spectrum between health and illness and an individual may slide from health into illness over a period of time and in a way that may be hard to identify. You do not catch mental illness and in general it is not amenable to tests or measurements but diagnostically is based on a careful assessment of symptoms and signs.

Why, then, do people become mentally ill? For some, particularly sufferers of the more serious illnesses, heredity has a part to play. There is no doubt that genetics influences susceptibility to illness but this by itself is not usually enough. The environment has an equally and for most a more important part to play in the development of illness. It is the context within which people are living their lives that is the key. How their individual personalities can manage the pressures and stresses of everyday living and the occurrence of negative or sometimes seemingly positive life events will dictate whether and when people cross the threshold from health into mental illness in its many forms.

In specialist psychiatric practice the emphasis is on predisposing, precipitating and perpetuating factors. The traditional medical approach to the diagnosis and management of mental illness is based on the rigid discipline of careful history taking including a history of the presenting complaint, a past medical and psychiatric history, a family and developmental history, consideration of social, forensic and substance misuse issues and an assessment of pre-morbid personality coupled with a thorough assessment of the mental state including appearance and general behaviour, mood, any abnormalities of thinking or perception including hallucinations and delusions, assessment of levels of suicide risk and of cognitive function and an assessment of degree of insight into the prevailing circumstances.

The specialist is in the privileged position of having a patient in front of them who has already been identified as having a problem or they would not be there. Equally, people are prepared to admit things in the confidential setting of the doctor's clinic that they might not admit to outside that setting.

The circumstance for the coach is a very different one. First of all they are more likely to see individuals who are in the prodrome of illness, a period that precedes the characteristic manifestations of the fully developed illness, rather than its acute or developed presentation. The relationship between coach and client is very different to the doctor–patient relationship and great care must be taken to avoid circumstances where the client's situation may be made worse by the wrong sort of intervention.

In this volume Andrew and Carole Buckley use their combined experiences as coach, counsellor and general practitioner to signpost the way to safe and effective coaching of the potentially vulnerable client. They provide an overview of the categories of mental illness, their definitions, epidemiology and management, techniques on the identification and recognition of the signs of mental illness using practical case-based examples and, most importantly, an understanding of the ethics, problems and pitfalls, warning signs and the importance of an appropriate professional boundary.

Most people who suffer from a mental illness will make a full recovery with the appropriate diagnosis, management and treatment. Doing what is right and, more importantly, not doing what is wrong is the cornerstone of good quality care for the psychiatrist, the general practitioner and the coach alike. This volume provides valuable insights into the complex and fascinating world of helping fellow human beings through what can be the most disabling and distressing of times. The rewards can be considerable for all concerned.

Read on!

Dr Mike P. Nowers FRCPsych
Consultant Psychiatrist

Introduction

by Andrew Buckley

In the early 1980s I was working for a pharmaceutical company and had an appointment in the department of psychiatry of a hospital. This was my first visit and I didn't know where I was going. The receptionist told me to go up to the fifth floor. I heard a voice over my shoulder saying 'I'm going there, I'll show you the way'. I was a bit nervous, not having any idea what to expect in a psychiatric hospital, although I had seen the film 'One Flew Over the Cuckoo's Nest' and was relieved that this well-dressed and groomed man was offering me assistance.

As we went over to the lift I realised that a scruffy man was following him, greasy hair pulled back in a ponytail and a grubby 'T' shirt with some banal phrase on it. I kept close to my saviour in the lift.

When all three of us got out at the fifth floor my saviour was escorted back through locked doors to a secure ward and I was left talking to the scruffy senior nurse, who was one of the people I was due to see.

When we meet someone with a physical disability or ailment there are outward signs that something is out of the ordinary and we can adjust our thoughts and actions appropriately. Whether this is a lifelong disability, the result of trauma or a temporary illness there are, often, visible signs that can be picked up on.

The sports coach has many advantages at the first meeting with a prospective client to life, executive and other psychologically based coaches. The sports coach can instantly see that this person has the physical form to be a shot-put champion but not a flat-race jockey. The sports coach can see whether the client looks reasonably healthy, not overweight, not out of breath just walking into the gym and can monitor this throughout the session. As a 'talking' coach we do not have these advantages. We cannot readily pick up clues that a bright middle manager has the resilience and fortitude to succeed at the highest commercial level and not be injured by coaching, nor can we see whether trying to coach an individual to reach personal targets will not be thwarted by their mental physique or previous injuries.

The challenge that this book sets out to address is how to allow these psychological issues to be as readily identified and dealt with as physical issues are for the sports coach.

There seems to be something almost sacred about having a sound mind; there is a far higher general acceptance of one or more parts of the body breaking down either temporarily or permanently than any suggestion that one's mind may not be fully functioning at the moment. When a friend or work colleague goes into hospital for an operation there is sympathy, flowers and support for the family but what is the general perception when someone is diagnosed with bipolar affective disorder or admitted to a treatment centre for addictions? Yet the lifetime risk of having a diagnosed mental health problem is probably about one in four. In the UK about 40 per cent of consultations with general medical practitioners are for psychiatric issues.

The prevalence of psychological problems is enormous and yet, in western society at least, there are still significant taboos and stigma attached to open acknowledgement that someone is mentally ill. These taboos can also extend into the professional field. The professional coach, welfare officer, mentor, human resource officer or learning and development manager may find it difficult to countenance that what is going on in the person they are talking to has its roots in mental illness or emotional disturbance. One of the aims of this book is to help open up this area so that possible psychological issues can be included as one of the options when things are not going as expected.

For example, a newly promoted female manager is really struggling to manage her team and becoming increasingly stressed. This could be a training issue – does she know how to delegate and manage others? She could be unsupported by her line manager and need help prioritising her efforts. Or, it could be a deep-seated inability to trust others, even, maybe, an inability to be assertive with her predominantly male team due to childhood abuse.

Alternatively, the successful male businessman is asking for coaching on relationships because 'they always go wrong'. Perhaps his relationships come to nothing because he has an undiagnosed form of autism and cannot be close to people. Alternatively, it may become clear that he has a tendency to talk of others as objects and be very controlling, signs of narcissistic personality disorder.

In both the above cases, coaching is likely to be, at best, ineffective, at worst, potentially damaging for the client. For the female manager, coaching towards effective management of team members, delegation skills, etc. may well reinforce her inability to trust others. She is likely to fail at tasks and plans, leading to a spiral of frustration, as she is unable to achieve reasonable goals. In a way this is similar to a golf coach trying to improve someone's swing, when that person has a frozen shoulder. If the coach does not identify that there is a physical reason why the coaching is not working, continuing to push against the pain in the shoulder could result in permanent damage; certainly the swing is not going to improve. The golfer may need to rest for a couple of weeks, go for help from a specialist, ask for medical intervention or maybe accept that they will never be able to play golf due to the limitations of movement in the shoulder.

When struggling to coach a golfer who is having problems with the swing the coach needs to assess whether this is a golfer with a problem or a problem golfer. A problem golfer can be coached. This is someone who may not be standing in the most effective way, not rotating shoulders, maybe using the wrong club. Issues to be coached. The golfer with a problem will not respond to coaching. The golfer with a problem is the person with the frozen shoulder, stiff back or similar and they will not benefit from coaching until the barrier to golfing has been dealt with.

Someone with a psychosocial, psychological or mental

health issue will follow a similar pattern. There is the problem client, the client with something they want to change or develop. There is the client with a problem, a problem that prevents effective coaching.

Once the client, the coach or other professional has identified that there is a barrier to achieving the goal there will be a similar range of options to the golf coach. The mental suffering may have a clear cause that is likely to go away in a few weeks without anything more than a pause in the coaching, through to a serious and possibly fatal prognosis that needs immediate emergency action. The options range from continuing to coach, with an awareness that there is a sensitive area, through coaching whilst the client receives other support (maybe from family and friends, maybe the medical profession), to stopping the coaching possibly with a view to resuming it in the future, supporting the client while they find other help or even initiating immediate emergency action.

The golf coach does not need to know what the problem in the shoulder is, they do not need to be able to diagnose a medical issue and suggest a course of treatment. It does not matter to the golf coach whether the problem is with a trapped nerve, a pulled muscle, damage to the joint or some other physical problem, the coach just needs to know that working on this person's golf swing needs to stop, at least for the moment.

The coach, human resources professional, mentor or employer has a similar focus and goal to the golf coach. Accurate diagnosis is not the goal, which should be left to the medical professionals.

What the coach needs is an ability to recognise when coaching isn't the whole solution and how to proceed in the best interests of the client. This requires:

- first, an awareness that some people will have temporary or more permanent mental health issues that will prove to be barriers to effective coaching;
- second, an ability to recognise the signs;
- third, the need to reflect on the ethics, legalities, practicalities and circumstances before,
- finally, choosing the best route forwards.

Table i.1 **Unusual behaviour?**

What could be happening?
Is the client upset?
Have they received bad news?
Or are these signs of mental illness?

The coach needs to know
What to look for
How to build a picture
What to do

To answer the questions
What is happening?
Is my client OK?
Should I coach or not?

How can this book help?

A Guide to Coaching and Mental Health is intended for experienced and inexperienced coaches and those using similar skills in their professional life, the human resources professional, mentor, employer, manager and others who find themselves with people who may show signs of mental illness. The intention is to provide a general background to the issues of working with people at an emotional or psychological level and an overview of the signs and symptoms seen in people experiencing problems. Once something has happened that arouses suspicion, the book shows how careful questioning can explore this and lead to an appropriate outcome.

Section 1 – Working on the boundary – starts by exploring the background to the issues. What is a normal feeling? What is an appropriate behaviour? Looking at what is generally considered normal behaviour allows the abnormal to be more easily seen. 'Normal' is a very difficult quality to categorise – what is OK in one environment may be clearly very strange in another; one person's negative is another person's positive. The effect of situations and context is explored. How behaviours are judged plays a crucial role in identifying potential issues: some people may judge a behaviour as perfectly normal and acceptable, even a real positive, that is viewed by others as totally bizarre or unacceptable. This holds true with both the views of the coach and views of the client.

These issues are explored in Chapter 1 before setting out a clear scheme of questioning in Chapter 2 that will help to gather information before the coach makes a choice as to the best way forward.

We approach what is going on from the clients' viewpoint, the coach's viewpoint and any third party viewpoint (the employer, for example, in business coaching), and from legal, ethical, moral and practical viewpoints in Chapter 3 before discussing the most appropriate routes forward in Chapter 4.

The primary question to answer is: should coaching continue?

Section 2 – What's being said? – uses fictional scenarios to develop realistic dialogues with clients. This highlights some of the warning signs and provides examples of questions that can explore the issues further. There are suggestions of ways forward to help explore the options available to the coach. Most of these scenarios develop in more than one way, demonstrating how similar starting points can lead to different conclusions and routes forward.

Section 3 – Categories of mental illness, their definition, epidemiology and management – provides a brief overview of the more common mental illnesses as defined medically.

The aim of this section is not to provide the facility for coaches and other related professionals to provide a diagnosis but to offer a different route to learning. It is inappropriate for a non-medically qualified person to offer a diagnosis but some knowledge of similarities and differences between medical diagnoses can help explore what is going on for the client and inform the decision-making process. By using this section, readers will gain insight into the variety of mental illnesses.

This book should not be read as the definitive guide to recognising and dealing with mental health problems; it is incomplete in many areas. However, it will provide sufficient insight into issues to allow those who may come across signs of mental illness in their professional capacities the ability to deal with most of them appropriately. A tentative label of a problem may be useful for the coach, particularly in discussions with others, but it is not a diagnosis. The book suggests what are commonly considered appropriate treatments for certain conditions, but is not a treatment guide for the coach to follow.

In the following chapters the reader will learn how to recognise the signs and symptoms that warrant further exploration and the factors to consider before deciding on the most appropriate way forward.

SECTION 1

Working on the boundary

Those working in a coaching capacity, and allied areas, will not have the daily exposure to mental health issues that a counsellor, therapist or medically qualified specialist has. Seeing the signs and symptoms of psychiatric problems will be the exception rather than the rule.

Early recognition of a problem is key to a positive outcome for the client. Early recognition is also key to a successful outcome for the coaching. For the coach this needs to be an ability to recognise signs, check them out and consider the most appropriate way forward. For the coaching to have a successful outcome does not necessarily mean that the coaching must be a success. The result of a successful coaching contract could be the recognition that coaching will not work, or that the client has some problem that needs another type of intervention.

However much exposure to and experience of mental health problems someone has, each case seen is unique and needs an individual evaluation before deciding on the way ahead. The following chapters go through this evaluation sequentially, starting with Chapter 1, exploring mental health issues within the context of a professional relationship. Chapter 2 looks at recognising the signs and how to explore these with a view to finding out enough information for the coach and client, working together in most cases, to start the decision-making process. Part of this decision making is a consideration of contractual obligations, ethical guidelines and the practicalities of how to continue, points covered in Chapter 3. The final chapter of Section 1, Chapter 4, looks into the choices faced by the coach and client for the future, ranging from continuing coaching to taking emergency action.

Developing a picture

The purpose of this book is to help with decisions around the appropriateness and likely effectiveness of a professional relationship with a client. However the relationship is defined – coach–client, welfare officer–colleague, mentor–mentee, human resources professional–employee, or manager–team member – the relationship has a purpose and reason for existing. Occasionally something will occur that suggests that the reasons for the relationship existing cannot be met due to a psychological issue. The reason for a relationship to exist between a coach and client is so that the client can benefit from the experience of being coached. If, for any reason – psychological, physical or practical – the client cannot enter into the relationship then it will fail to achieve any expected benefit. If, for any reason, an issue arises during the course of the relationship that proves to be a barrier to effective coaching then there will be no benefit to the relationship.

Coaching is a 'helping by talking' relationship (Bachkirova and Cox 2004: 1) and has many links and similarities to counselling, psychotherapy and other talking relationships. One contrast often used to describe the difference between coaching and counselling or psychotherapy is that the coach works with a clinically well population from the perspective of mental health and that the counsellor or therapist works with identifiable dysfunctions. Without joining the debate as to the accuracy of this statement the assumption of the basic 'wellness' of the client is a powerful starting point in the coach–client relationship. This basic wellness is also an appropriate starting point in manager–employee and other such relationships. But it is an assumption only and is unlikely to be checked out in advance. An assumption of the mental health of clients then makes it difficult to enter into conversations about past psychological history before coaching commences because questioning puts the basic assumption in doubt.

There are those that advocate a pre-coaching psychological assessment, for example Berglas says: 'At a minimum, every executive slated to receive coaching should first receive a psychological evaluation' (Berglas 2002: 92). The Chartered Institute of Personnel and Development in the UK acknowledges that there are those that will not benefit from coaching for psychological reasons but does not go so far as to recommend a formal pre-coaching assessment (Jarvis 2004: 36–38).

In most settings the assessment of the value of coaching is likely to be left to the coach and client to decide during their first meeting. This is particularly the case when the client has instigated coaching for themselves rather than an organisation suggesting coaching as a part of a personal development programme. The coach will be entering into a relationship with the hope that the client is mentally healthy but with no certainty or evidence to back this up.

The assumption is based on an absence of evidence rather than a clear measure of a person's health. People who have spent time with someone who has been labelled as mentally ill will know that, even in severe cases, there are long periods when the person appears to be acting normally and functioning appropriately.

The first task is to explore the difference between a 'normally functioning' individual and someone with mental health issues, and, of equal importance, the changes in an individual who is functioning normally today but may have problems tomorrow. This is the boundary when normal psychological functioning slips into some negative emotionally driven feelings and behaviours that cause distress to the individual or reduce their ability to perform the tasks needed. The starting point is an exploration of what is normal, followed by signs that may suggest that something is abnormal and then how to conceptualise these potential abnormalities to help define the choices available. One of the hardest decisions faced by the coach or other professional when dealing with someone who has shown some signs of psychological issue or emotional distress is to decide what impact this will have on the relationship and the specific goals of the relationship. The final part of this chapter – 'They were OK when I started' – provides a framework to define the type of issue that the client may have and how this may impact on any further coaching.

What is normal?

A clear statement that a person is mentally healthy is difficult; the best that will be achieved by any professional is 'no signs of psychological dysfunction are evident', which is not the same as an unequivocal statement that this person is mentally healthy.

When thinking about the relative wellness of the human psyche and personality a clear yes or no choice will be the exception. Within the medical profession there is little consensus when dealing with psychological issues. One doctor's reading of a set of symptoms can lead to medication, another, viewing the same patient, may decide on a suggestion of a 'talking therapy', whilst yet another may refer to a psychiatrist; there is always the choice of doing nothing, maybe with the thought that there is nothing out of the ordinary. Science can provide little help in diagnosing mental health issues; physical measurements are not available in this branch of medicine as they are in cardiology, for example. The diagnosis and treatment suggestions are more of an art than a science. The relative 'wellness' – 'illness' of the patient is a changeable boundary that can vary from day to day.

To come to a conclusion as to what is normal behaviour and what is appropriate behaviour it will be helpful to explore the boundary area in a general way. The boundary between mental health and mental illness is unclear; the most likely time that the boundary is defined is when someone is diagnosed, and hence labelled, with a specific illness. There are many people who will go through long periods of behaving strangely, or being 'under the weather' who would be diagnosed with a psychological problem if seen by a doctor.

A definition of mental health relies more on an ability to function appropriately than a measure of healthiness or even normality.

Functioning appropriately relies on a context and a judgement of what is appropriate rather than any globally acceptable scale of 'health'. For example, the commonest psychological issue that doctors see is depression and yet depressing can be a very appropriate behavioural choice for all human beings, for example a feeling of hopelessness and despair when you come upon a queue of traffic unexpectedly, and realise you will be late for an appointment, perhaps with guilt that 'I should have left earlier', maybe sadness that you are not going to get to your destination on time. Depressing is a reasonable and appropriate antidote to stress in everyday activities, and the inability to choose depressing as an option allows the opposing feelings of anger, agitation, etc. the freedom to come to the fore unchecked and leads to a far more stressful situation.

Figure 1.1 shows a normal or Gaussian curve of the amount of depressing used by individuals in the population. A few people have lots of severe symptoms; some people have few, if any, symptoms. Most people are in the middle, most of the time. Those at the right end of the scale will be unable to function appropriately due to their depression, those at the left are not using depressing as a coping strategy and will be prone to experiencing high stress levels, anxiety and anger in certain situations when most would use temporary depression as a suitable response.

Emotional intelligence has become popular in recent years as a way of describing the emotionally functioning person: a person who is labelled as 'OK' is someone who has realistic control over their emotions, they use emotions appropriately, neither denying them nor being flooded by them. This position equates to the central position in the curve shown in Figure 1.1.

The shoulders of the curve are the areas where problems are likely to occur that need to be identified and explored

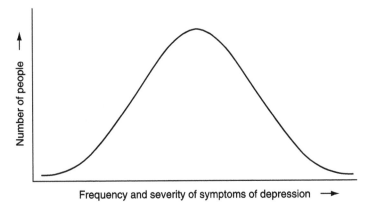

Figure 1.1 The normal curve of distribution of symptoms throughout the population

during coaching, where depressing is being used both appropriately and inappropriately and affecting the client's life and ability to achieve.

It is the strength, frequency and severity of the symptom that is the important pointer to a diagnosis of depression, not the symptom in isolation.

A similar pattern can be seen through most, if not all, of the range of psychological problems. In a study by Belinda Board and Katarina Fritzon (2005) titled 'Disordered personalities at work', the authors write: 'there are good grounds to argue for an approach that observes characteristics of PDs [Personality Disorders] as simply exaggerated forms of normal behaviour' (p. 18). They go on to show that a sample of senior business managers had many similar traits of psychopathic personality disorder to those in a high security mental hospital and under psychiatric care.

Despite the attention-grabbing title to this paper the conclusion is further evidence that the symptoms of mental illness, particularly psychopathic personality disorder in this case, are best viewed as on a continuum rather than as a discreet have or have not; the problem comes from the exaggeration of the behaviour and how the behaviour impacts on the person's life.

However attractive the proposition may be to some employees, the purpose of this example is not to suggest that senior managers are psychopaths and should be locked up, but that some of the traits routinely used to identify and categorise the psychopathic personality disorder are as prevalent in a 'normal' population as those with serious mental illness. The signs of mental illness are all around.

The simplistic concept of symptoms as a way to identify those with psychological, psychosocial or mental health problems will not help in any but the most severe and obvious of cases. Even with what is termed 'gross pathology', very clear symptoms and context must be included before a diagnosis. The World Health Organization puts 'hallucinations, e.g. hearing voices when no one is around' at the top of its list of presenting complaints for acute psychotic disorders (WHO 2000: 15) but, would you suggest that a priest who talks of listening to the voice of God be so diagnosed?

Section 3 lists symptoms that medical practitioners use to help identify and choose the treatment for those suffering from mental illness. Many symptoms are repeated between illness groups and many of the symptoms can appear perfectly normal, common and usual when viewed in isolation. Hallucinating seems quite a strong, clear, indicator of a problem, but what about dreams? How real these can appear even after becoming fully awake. How many people have 'seen' a deceased love one sitting in their favourite chair upon entering a room, or 'felt' the pressure of a faithful pet on their leg long after the pet has passed away? These two examples can be classed as hallucinations; the difference to the psychotic is the transitory nature of 'knowing it is real'.

The context, the specific environment, the feelings, the beliefs and thoughts around what is happening influence the judging of the behaviour. The normality of the behaviour is judged in its social context, what is normal for this society at this time and society can be anything from a nation, a business, the family to a group of friends. Judging someone else's behaviours brings in its own problems – the judge's own belief system of the normality of this behaviour and, if the behaviour is not normal, is it beneficial or to be applauded in some way?

Addiction is a negative term to most people, commonly linked to the use of various drugs and chemicals. Some may extend the term to alcohol, tobacco and gambling. Perhaps fewer people may be comfortable including sex and food in the list of addictive behaviours. Similarly with obsessions and compulsions, they tend to be viewed as a negative. Obsessed with checking that doors are locked, compulsively washing hands, obsessively playing computer games, compulsively planning the day to watch a specific television programme, the list is endless, with a common factor that those involved in the activity feel varying degrees of discomfort when they cannot carry out the behaviour.

The addictive, obsessive and compulsive personality reports feeling uncomfortable or distressed when their chosen activity is denied them for whatever reason. But what of the runner? The person who jogs most mornings as routine will often report a need to run when they have been unable to follow their routine for some reason. Those who meditate regularly are reported as saying that they feel uncomfortable and 'not right' when this is denied them. Every so often there is a report in the press of some sporting success followed by a story of how the sportsperson would spend hour after hour practising. The footballer kicking for goal for hours at a time, the batsperson swinging the bat and hitting balls. Similarly with musicians, there is a new virtuoso on the block, or a young musician wins an award and the reports include the number of hours spent practising for the last 15 years. There are complaints in the press of the hours that parents allow their children to play computer games, but seldom comments about a teenager playing the piano for five or six hours a day, not unusual for anyone who becomes a top-class pianist. The only difference in psychological terms to both these two obsessive behaviours are the material the keys are made of and society's view of the benefit.

William Glasser wrote about this in the book *Positive addiction* (Glasser 1976), highlighting the similarities between the activities commonly called addictions and these other activities that show very similar traits, but have what society has chosen as a positive outcome, and seem to be a positive for the 'addicted' person. Psychologically the issue of becoming set in a routine is very similar for the alcoholic and the runner, the person who meditates and the obsessive-compulsive.

The coach is likely to meet clients who show behaviours that, if they are denied, they become uncomfortable. The ability of a top-class salesperson to continue to make sales calls is applauded in many companies; this person is held up as a role model. The successful salesperson may show many signs of obsessive behaviour – not trusting anyone else to speak to their clients, suspicion that someone is trying to steal contacts, a difficulty focusing on anything other than the act of selling, the need to sell coming before anything else, even family and loved ones. This is an obsession with the sale, success and reward and can lead to problems of stress and burnout as well as relationship difficulties in both personal and professional life. If the activity is denied, during a holiday for example, then this type of salesperson is likely to become increasingly irritable and prone to turning to another activity to meet the need to get the 'buzz' denied them. The need to control their feelings could be met by using alcohol or another drug, an activity to get the adrenaline pumping or something competitive where feelings can be changed by winning. They may be prone to periods of low mood or depression. This type of salesperson will be successful whilst selling but could develop psychological problems beyond the scope of coaching if promoted to team leader or manager, a move that would make it harder to meet the psychological needs that have become addictive and have been met by the selling process.

Where does normal become abnormal or a helpful behaviour become unhelpful? There seems to be neither clear consensus nor a simple means of testing this, as everyone is unique, both in psychological make-up and in how the environment affects them. In a challenging situation some people will 'rise to the challenge' and others will be destroyed by it. Some idea of the likely behaviour that people will show under challenging circumstances can be gleaned from examining past behaviours, but until the experience has happened no one can be certain how people will respond. The human psyche does not readily fit into categories, it inhabits the grey area of uncertainty, irrationality and variation. To some, viewing humans as rational creatures is attractive, but humans behave emotionally first and rationally second. A bold statement perhaps, but backed up by the Nobel Prize for Economics being presented to Daniel Kahneman in 2002. This eminent Professor of Psychology, in collaboration with others, evidenced the emotional primacy of human decision making to the satisfaction of the prize-winning committee. Those who work with others around emotional areas, from teachers to sports coaches, managers to psychotherapists, will know that people make decisions that appear bizarre to others, no two people will respond the same way, what motivates one person will demotivate another and other such anachronisms of humanity. Without the emotional variety of human nature there would be no coaching. A simple instruction would lead to a known and predictable outcome, and repeating an instruction would always give the same outcome.

The impossibility of defining 'normal' in a clear and unequivocal way leaves the coach in a position of having to assume this state until proven otherwise. But the abnormal does appear and must be dealt with; denying it, minimising its importance or relying on others to notice problems will lead to situations that could be damaging and dangerous for both the client and coach.

How to spot what is abnormal

So far the variety, variation and unpredictability of the human psyche has been explored, how normal behaviour is an elusive state and that abnormal behaviours can be seen every day. The context of this book is the boundary between healthy and unhealthy psychology, and what to do about it when the signs occur in a professional relationship.

Occasionally the signs will be self-evident as with Carl in Chapter 7 and Ghulam in Chapter 11; more often, vague and insubstantial but, nevertheless, present. Most commonly it will be an accumulation of signs, changing behaviours and puzzling responses that will alert the coach to a possible issue that needs exploration.

Table 1.1 **Signs to look for**

Watch out for:

Appearance
- Unkempt?
- Unusual?
- Body language, movement?

Behaviour
- Agitated?
- Uninterested?
- Evasive?
- Incongruent behaviour?

Mood
- Apathetic?
- Sad or hopeless?
- Inappropriately optimistic?
- Overly pessimistic?

Thoughts
- Preoccupations?
- Fixated?
- Irrational?
- Delusional?

Perception
- Hallucinations?
- Unreal experiences?
- An abnormal viewpoint?

Intellect
- Not as expected?
- Changes?
- Not 'present'?

A whole range of signs can alert the coach to an issue, some are listed in Table 1.1. It is particularly important to note any changes over time with a client and any signs that are incongruent with the expected. Broadly speaking, the signs to be aware of fall into seven areas:

- *Appearance* – with regard to dress and grooming, has the client dressed unusually, perhaps carelessly, or is there evidence of lack of personal care with dirty clothes or unwashed appearance? Is there anything out of the ordinary in the way the client moves or doesn't, or unusual, maybe inappropriate body language?

- *Behaviour* – does the client appear agitated and nervous, or lethargic and uninterested? Are there any visible signs such as sweating or repetitive behaviours? Are they cooperative or aggressive? Does their facial expression match up with what is being said or discussed?
- *Mood* – is it optimistic or pessimistic? This is of particular note if it doesn't correlate with other information. Similarly, does the client's mood seem to be at odds with what they are saying? Is the client active, emotionally, behaviourally and physically or fixed, inactive, possibly apathetic?
- *Thoughts* – does the client talk of any particular preoccupations, over and over, perhaps there appears to be a fixation on one topic or thought? Are thoughts, as expressed, reasonably rational or do some thoughts appear irrational or delusional?
- *Perception* – are there signs that suggest that the client is not experiencing a normal world? This is experiencing as 'real' something that is not, i.e. an hallucination and can be seeing something, hearing something, smelling something, tasting something or experiencing touch in an abnormal way.
- *Intellect* – does the client appear to be as expected intellectually? The coach may notice a change over time in the client's intellectual abilities that needs exploring. Are there signs that the client is 'not really here' today, something about them suggesting that they are not present and taking part in the session?
- *Insight* – can the client offer an explanation for these unusual signs? Does the explanation or how the client attributes the unusual signs seem reasonable?

None of these signs shows mental illness when viewed in isolation. Even something as worrying as an hallucination may have a reasonable cause. A viral illness or Malaria can produce hallucinations; it could, just possibly, be that the client inadvertently took the latest designer drug while out the night before and the hallucinations are the hangover of that event.

How abnormal is it really?

The signs and symptoms of mental illness are explored in detail in Sections 2 and 3 of this book. They form patterns and shapes of behaviour that come together to suggest, initially, a cause and then a solution. Mental health professionals sometimes grade categories of illness on severity, with personality disorders and character traits at the lowest level, with neurosis such as anxiety, phobias and panic attacks next, followed by depression, then psychoses and mania, with schizophrenia, dementia and delirium at the severe end of the scale. Another way of categorising psychological, psychosocial and mental health problems is to group them around the type of suffering experienced.

The three categories that may prove useful are functional suffering, dysfunctional suffering and mental illness. Again, these are not distinct and separate states, nor a straightforward continuum. Best viewed as a grouping of interlinked circles with areas of overlap (see Figure 1.2), they provide a useful pointer when deciding on a course of action. Thinking about the type of problem in this way can be helpful, because the goal is not an accurate diagnosis but an effective outcome to the coaching. Being able to differentiate the type of problem the client is experiencing is an important part of the decision-making process.

Functional suffering

First, is the suffering, or pain, associated with an identifiable event such as bereavement, loss or a traumatic event? This is functional suffering, the type of emotional pain or distress that would appear normal and usual in the circumstances. However distressing, debilitating or horrible this suffering is to experience or observe, it is normal. Just because suffering looks like it is normal and appropriate it does not follow that it can be ignored. The person experiencing functional

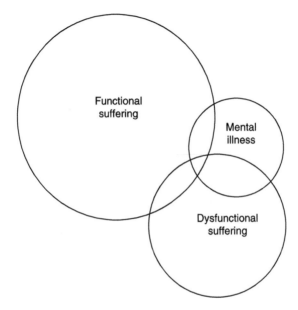

Figure 1.2 Categories of problems

suffering can be experiencing high levels of emotional pain and their functioning is likely to be impaired, certainly the client's ability to engage in coaching will be affected.

Functional suffering can be triggered by many life events and be short lived, but nevertheless intense, or last for months or years. The spectrum ranges from events that impact on one coaching session to something that suggests that coaching either should not start or be terminated and more appropriate support sought promptly. Anger around a damaged car or other possession, a setback at work, an argument with a loved one or work colleague can all lead to functional suffering. In the run up to an anxiety-inducing event some people will find their ability to function severely impaired so that coaching, or other relationships, will be ineffective. The fairy-story ideal of approaching marriage is of joy and excitement but many people experience heightened anxiety, even paralysing fear, combined with unusual behaviour: forgetfulness, inability to complete tasks, irritability, grandiose gestures, indecisiveness, the list is endless and subject of many works of fiction. A life or personal coach may be able to provide a useful anchor in these circumstances but business coaching is likely to be ineffective.

A potential mistake that could be made when a client is suffering due to an identifiable event could be to judge the feelings that the client has from a general viewpoint of what would be a normal feeling. For example, if a parent dies, the generally held belief is that the child, of whatever age, will grieve the parent and be saddened by the loss. This may not be the case; the client may be pleased that their parent has died and feel guilty about these feelings, leading to a very difficult time for them. This could be far more than relief that suffering is over for an elderly parent after a long illness, because the client actively hates their mother or father – not everyone receives good parenting and not everyone follows the generally accepted rule of loving their parents. Something similar could happen after a promotion. The generally held view would be that this is a positive event, the client may show signs of pleasure that conform to society's norms but, inwardly, hate the idea and have felt pressured to look for promotion as a way of conforming.

A mismatch between what is being felt and what the expected feelings should be can be a substantial, maybe total, block to any coaching efforts. In a business context the expected norm is that the owners and key stakeholders will want to grow the business but trying to coach a board member who really wants the company to stay a small, fun, place to work will be ineffective, and the client may find the need to pretend to want to work towards growth very disturbing and could exhibit any of a variety of signs and symptoms of mental health problems. This client is showing signs of functional suffering because the process of looking at change that they do not want is at the bottom of their emotional disturbance.

During the period after major life-changing events, clients may experience functional suffering as new circumstances are adjusted to. A client stepping outside their comfort zone into a new and challenging position may experience more than concerns and worries as they rise to the challenge. The nature of the new responsibilities could lead to panic attacks, depression or inappropriate use of alcohol to cope with the feelings, of inadequacy for example. The new environment has caused some psychological stress and the client may need time to adjust, some support or to move out of the environment.

The environment, the combination of the physical space and the other people around, can cause functional suffering. Someone who is used to working in a small, light and airy office in a pleasant part of town may struggle if they change jobs to an open office in a tower block in the centre of a major city. They may adjust to this or the advantages of the new position may help them come to terms with the stress of the move but others may need to leave and find more suitable employment to remove the psychological stress. The coach may meet clients who cannot adjust to a new culture and no amount of coaching will help, except in helping the client realise they may need to move.

As coaching gains in acceptance and popularity and is seen as a potentially beneficial performance management tool there is likely to be an increasing call for remedial coaching, coaching the poor performer, or coaching to solve an issue. Some of these clients are likely to show signs of poor psychological functioning and the coach will be challenged to decide whether what they can offer will be beneficial. The technical expert, or top salesperson, promoted to manager are examples where psychological barriers may lead to an inability to function as an effective manager.

The common theme in the above examples is change; it is the change in circumstances that has triggered the suffering.

A client may approach a coach or have coaching suggested with the hope that problems in the 'system' can be resolved. The system could be an organisation, team or family. In a 'system' a person can be chosen as, or take on the role of, a scapegoat and labelled as the one with the problem, but when the coach gets to know them it becomes clear that there is little to be done because the system needs to change, not the individual. The client is struggling due to the behaviour of others. The stress caused by bullying, for example, which leads to poor performance, is unlikely to be coached away.

Similarly with a private client working on whole-life issues, there may be real functional suffering due to a relationship or the environment, where what is needed is not coaching, strategies, goal setting, reframing but a change of environment. Someone who has moved to a new culture, maybe a new country, may have experienced years of low-grade problems, a client in a dysfunctional relationship could be severely emotionally disturbed, neither are that likely to benefit from coaching except for the supportive relationship.

All these examples have a common theme of an identifiable current reason for experiencing mental health issues. It is the individual's reaction to their environment and relationships that is at the root of the problem, not a mental illness.

Dysfunctional suffering

Having a second classification of psychological suffering helps in the process of deciding what to do by helping the coach, or other professional, define what is behind the signs and symptoms that are causing concern. The first point of reference is seeing or hearing something that is unusual, when warning bells start to ring and the coach needs to decide what to do. Having an ability to roughly box things in will start to suggest a solution.

Dysfunctional suffering can be thought of as when the psychological distress does not have a focus based on what is really happening today. Or, when the reaction to the event seems considerably greater than what would normally be expected. It is an arbitrary definition, rather than one based on set guidelines, and its usefulness is as part of the decision-making process rather than as a diagnosis. From the perspective of the coach meeting a client, most inexplicable barriers to the coaching will be best classed as dysfunctional suffering. This is the area where experienced psychological help will be most often indicated – referral to a psychotherapist or mental health professional for another view of what is going on for the client – because it is this area that coaching may be most harmful to the client. One way of conceptualising this area of dysfunctional suffering is to imagine a person who has developed over the years an effective means of coping with, or covering up, psychological distress and the new suffering comes about because the old coping strategy no longer works. It is the area of childhood trauma, poor parenting, not being able to grow up in a psychologically healthy way, not being able to become an 'individual', living a life for someone else (most commonly a parent). Something changes for the person and the effective way of living that has been built up over the years no longer works.

Fundamentally, coaching is about change and change is one of the key triggers for dysfunctional suffering to emerge. Coaching seems to have fewer stigmas than counselling, psychotherapy and psychiatry and can attract the client who is suffering emotionally who views it as a more acceptable route to help. This could equally be the case with life and personal coaching as executive or business coaching. The struggling executive may be offered coaching as an easier option than a psychiatric referral, or even acceptance by the organisation that the client has been appointed in error and is not capable of handling the role for which they have been chosen.

One of the commonest reasons for coaching to be suggested or for a client to approach a coach is that something has changed. This could be enforced change, freely chosen change or routine change due to life's progression. Change means leaving something behind and moving on to new experiences. Both of these can be triggers, in some, for the emergence or re-emergence of psychological suffering. Moving on may remove the safety net that has been crafted over the years to allow the person to live a comfortable life. Alternatively, moving on to a new environment may bring out a character trait that has been hidden, or bring to the surface some old issues.

In the context of coaching, some form of psychological distress could become evident due to the action of coaching. The client may have specific issues relating to the goals of coaching that would not be causing problems without coaching. The client may be fully functioning in other areas of their life and have the desire to achieve more in their chosen area, but have specific barriers of psychological origin that coaching will not address. Some people will struggle to become team players because they are more comfortable when working alone, similarly there could be a great desire to be in a relationship, but being in a relationship causes psychological stress. Many people dream of running their own business, perhaps a lifestyle business based on a hobby or area of particular expertise. They may approach a coach for help but if this person is unable to self-motivate they are unlikely to succeed. It may be that their life has been structured around working in places where they have clear guidelines and expectations, they may achieve quite a lot whilst working with the coach, but it all falls down when the coaching finishes. These examples are areas where there are psychological barriers to achieving the expected results of the coaching, there may not be emotional distress or clear signs of issues but the client has a psychological barrier between where they are now and the goal that coaching is trying to help them get to.

Most people are able to adjust to life's changes, maybe with a little support from friends, family or work colleagues. Some people will find their lives severely disrupted and their day-to-day functioning impaired by a similar change. Trying to coach such a person can be ineffective or even harmful. It is analogous to a physical injury where activity or exercise can make an underlying physical complaint worse, leading to an injury taking far longer to heal or even leading to permanent disability.

The range of issues that the coach may face is enormous as can be seen by the scenarios in Section 2 and the discussions on classifications of mental illness in Section 3. The most important point for the coach is a recognition that any client may start to show signs of dysfunctional suffering at any time. The highly effective and successful businessman who 'loses his touch' after the death of his father – it may not be due to grieving but that there is no one left to achieve for, the need to win has gone. The competent and outwardly 'normal' woman who starts to drink heavily just after her 52nd birthday – it comes out that her mother died at the age of 53. The middle manager who becomes ineffective when a new female boss takes over the department – he cannot relate to women in authority because they remind him of his mother. Throughout this book are examples of dysfunctional suffering that the coach may come across; the list is endless and is probably the major barrier to effective coaching.

Mental illness

The third of the categories of psychological suffering is also more of an aid to choosing how to proceed with a client than a distinct diagnosis. It may sound as if this category is the one that can be clearly defined, by reference to standard classifications and lists of symptoms such as DSM IV (Diagnostic and Statistical Manual of Mental Disorders – Fourth Edition, WHO 1994), but it is an art and relies on the judgement of the medical practitioner involved. For the purpose of choosing how to proceed with a client showing signs of psychological problems, thoughts that the client may have a mental illness suggest a need for help from a mental health professional. The diagnosis of a mental illness is the province of the medical profession and hence, it follows that mental illness is a definition of the medical profession and is more an aid to treatment that a strict criteria. There is considerable overlap between mental illness and dysfunctional suffering, and even functional suffering. The choice of where to place someone in these groups lies with the person making the judgement.

For some people, being diagnosed, or labelled as suffering from a specific illness, can be a very positive experience. There is now a reason for the feelings and behaviours and, in a way, something to work with. Others may be happy with the diagnosis as it removes responsibility: 'I can't do anything, I'm depressed.' Treatment can only be forced on the individual in the most extreme cases and it can often be a waiting game for the doctor, trying to help the patient to accept the need for treatment. Talking therapies have little chance of success without the active participation of the client and compliance with drug treatment regimes is virtually impossible to force on an unwilling patient.

The relevance of these three classifications, which may appear very arbitrary at first glance, is as an aid to the coach, or other professional, in deciding what to do. The sporting analogy may be of further help; take the golf coach and the client with the frozen shoulder. First comes the recognition of pain and reduced movement followed by some exploratory questioning, which can lead to a rough classification of the problem from the perspective of the coach and coaching the client to play golf.

Functional suffering – recent injury, possibly a clear cause, most likely to go away in a short time. The coach either holds back on any more lessons until the pain has gone, or, maybe, focuses on putting, with the client's agreement, as an appropriate use of the time that meets the client's needs and does not impact on the shoulder.

Dysfunctional suffering – recognition that the client cannot move their shoulder correctly to swing the club. Pain may or may not be present, but the goal of coaching the golf swing will not be met. This could be an old injury, or of unknown origin. It could be that the pain seems to be in the shoulder but is really all about feeling giddy when the head is swung round. What the golf coach can do is limited by what the client wants. The coach could just work on putting, if that meets the client's needs, or suggest some medical help. It could be that the client has to give up on any idea of playing golf.

Mental illness – in the context of the golfing analogy, this would be a clear sign that something serious is wrong, and the coach will not go any further until someone appropriate has given the all clear. It may be that with correct supervision of the underlying problem the golf coaching could continue, the client may benefit from sensible exercise, but this would be coaching under medical supervision.

Both the golf coach and the psychological coach could meet clients who choose to ignore or mask a problem. With golfing this would be the golfer who plays despite being in pain, maybe fully aware that they will have several days of incapacity afterwards, or the golfer who takes painkillers to mask the pain. Both of these become ethical issues for the coach if they become aware of them. Similarly, the psychological coach may become aware of issues and areas that the client ignores or tries to cover up and will have to make a decision on how to proceed.

They were OK when I started

The evidence that a client has some form of mental health issue may come to light at the first meeting or after some time. Coaching that has been progressing satisfactorily for a number of sessions could quite unexpectedly become stuck due to a psychological issue or the client could start to show worrying signs of mental illness. There is a possibility that the act of coaching could be a trigger to mental illness, as coaching is about change and a client could be in an OK place before coaching and then become out of balance. Any change can be a trigger to a previously unseen mental health issue that the client may or may not have been aware of. The act of coaching, of behaving and questioning in certain ways, could bring to the surface signs of problems that the client may either not have been aware of or have thought were well hidden.

If the coach were to stop at the first hint of an upset, the first sign of anger or distress, the first difficulty that the client has in reaching a goal, then little, if any, coaching would occur. For most clients, coaching is challenging, often hard work, sometimes a struggle, rarely a smooth and peaceful journey. There will be occasions when it will be ineffective or potentially damaging to the client to carry on.

The act of coaching has a goal of extending and expanding a client's range of behaviours into new areas to enhance their life. By this very definition the client will be being asked to move out of their comfort zone, a tried and tested way of being where the client is familiar with how they will behave in most circumstances and will be able to maintain their position as a 'normal' person. Outside the comfort zone is unknown territory and potentially psychologically hostile.

Every psychological theory of human behaviour and development has an underlying theory of personality and motivation, a theory of change and how it is brought about and includes a view on how psychological damage occurs

and ways to recover from this. Coaching theory draws heavily on this tradition. It is beyond the goals of this book to
discuss any of these theories in depth but a concept of
change is needed to be able to help with the process of identifying, judging, categorising and evaluating signs that may
be an issue or barrier to effective coaching. What is needed is
a way of helping with the process of decision making with
the client who has shown some signs of mental illness.
A simple list of barriers to coaching would not work: what
is a barrier to one person will be inconsequential to another.
Similarly, a description of possible psychological traumas
and how these could theoretically impact on coaching
would be meaningless as every single potential client is so
unique.

What follows is an attempt to paint a picture that gives
an insight into how clients may find problems during their
coaching journey.

The human personality develops and changes throughout life, from the tiniest baby to the most senior, senior
citizen, it never stops. All life experiences come together to
make up the unique personality of the individual and how
they choose to behave in all situations. These experiences
take the individual to a natural place where they feel
balanced and in control – the comfort zone. No one would
consider leaving this place unless it had become uncomfortable in some way, or they could see, quite close by (i.e.
achievable), a more pleasant-looking place. This movement
from one place to another is the central tenet of coaching.

An individual's route to their comfort zone will be influenced by positive and negative life experiences that have
steered them to their present destination. They move towards
the positive and away from the negative throughout life.

People inhabit their particular comfort zone because it
meets their needs, or it used to meet their needs or, for some,
it gives the illusion of meeting their needs. Probably the
majority of any population are happy enough in their comfort zones and will stay there, with a few bits of redecora-
tion, for the rest of their lives. They have found a place where
they can continue to get their needs met. Thankfully, for the
coaching industry, some people want something different

and want help to find the way. These are prospective coaching clients. There will be those whose zone is more of a discomfort than a comfort who may approach a coach for a variety of reasons, thinking this will help. Both those happy in their zones and those who are really in a discomfort zone may have coaching 'suggested' by others who want them to change or think it is for the best.

The first difference for the coach to think of is whether the client is in a comfort zone that is no longer meeting their needs fully, and they want to move, or in a discomfort zone.

The term 'discomfort zone' is used to describe someone who is showing signs that suggest a mental health problem. The purpose of this book is to help identify and take appropriate action when the coach meets a client in a discomfort zone. The coach does not attempt to move a client in a discomfort zone but may help them to recognise and accept this and to take a more appropriate course of action.

- When a client seems to be in a discomfort zone when you first meet them, do not coach them but help them to find more appropriate forms of help.

It is not by chance that people end up where they are, psychologically; it is the end result of years of moving along, away from negatives and towards positives, or away from the unfamiliar and towards the familiar. The second type of client who may need attention for psychological problems are those who, at first meeting, are absolutely OK, or certainly appear so, but who have hidden problems which become evident during the course of coaching. This is the person who functions comfortably and appropriately in the comfort zone, but may live here because it is safe, as there are traps and barriers just outside which could lead to upset. If the action of coaching moves someone from a comfort zone to a discomfort zone then the coach and client need to address the issue and work out an appropriate way forward.

- If a client moves into a discomfort zone during coaching, reassess the focus and direction before deciding whether to continue or to look for more appropriate help.

To help with this process of reassessment it will be useful to build an approximation of the likely impact on the coaching of the issue that has arisen. An overly cautious approach would be to stop coaching and refer any client who showed the first sign of a psychological problem; this would not always be in the best interests of the client, the coach or any third party organisation involved. An overly optimistic approach, ignoring any signs and carrying on regardless, will lead to serious consequences in the future.

Thinking about the type of issue that has appeared and the likely effect this may have on the future of the coaching will lead to more balanced decisions being taken. A good starting point is to pose the question: 'what is the goal of the coaching?', and this will lead to one of two possible answers:

1 The client wishes to move to a new zone, and become comfortable in it.
2 The client wishes to expand their present zone.

This is overly simplistic as a goal for coaching, but is appropriate in the context of dealing with the signs of psychological stress, distress and mental illness. With choice 1 (above) there has been a change for the client and they are looking for help in functioning in the new environment. This could be the newly promoted manager, whose present comfort zone is as technical expert and needs coaching to be successful in the new area of people management, delegation and strategic thinking or the person whose life has changed, due, for example, to a divorce, children leaving home or a change in career, who wants to look at the options for their future. Choice 2 is the successful executive who is interested in developing themselves further in their present role to become more self-aware and increase the range of behavioural options they have available, or, the client who is feeling unfulfilled, although generally happy, with their present comfort zone and wishes to include new experiences and new ways of behaving to enhance what they have already got. These two choices are shown in Figure 1.3.

The problems of a psychological nature that the client may find and the coach may need to decipher and make choices around lie in the areas covered by the arrows in

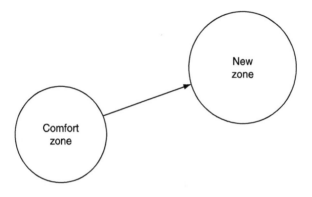

Choice 1 – a new zone

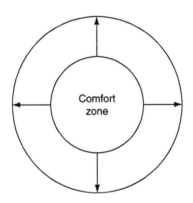

Choice 2 – an expanded zone

Figure 1.3 **Coaching goals**

Figure 1.3, the direction of movement that the client wants to make. These problems are infinite in their variety, their effect on the client in the short and long term and the impact they have on coaching. They can, however, be broken down theoretically to help with the decision-making process:

- Barriers
- Traps

- Turbulence
- Minefields.

Barriers

Barriers are an effective block to any coaching. When a barrier is present along the line that the direction of the coaching needs to take (an arrow in Figure 1.3) it is like meeting a brick wall and the client can go no further in that direction. The key words are 'in that direction'. A barrier does not mean that a client necessarily has a mental illness; it means that there is something in the way of the route to achieving a specified goal.

A barrier can be sidestepped or compensated for (see Figure 1.4) and coaching can be effective and productive simply by adjusting the goals to allow for the problem area. A barrier can be retreated from; if a client meets a psychological barrier during the course of coaching they may choose to back away from it. The client may choose to address the difficulties presented by the barrier in the future or change their expectations to compensate for this difficult area in their lives.

An example of a barrier to coaching would be the executive who is using a coach to improve general performance and increase effectiveness. One part of this is looking at relationships where it becomes clear that there is little warmth in any work-based relationships and these are superficial, transactionally based. This is a barrier to coaching in this area irrespective of whether the client is unable to look at relating at a more personal level (fear of being close to others for example) or does not see any need to have a warmer, more empathetic, relationship. It may be possible to meet the client's goals by compensating for this (Figure 1.4).

Another example would be the client who wants to set up their own business, where fear of failure is a barrier. This client may be able to sidestep the barrier by working towards a temporary position, which is less risky, such as combining the new venture with a part-time job.

With the case of Carl in Chapter 7, either of the first two scenarios presented in the chapter, of Asperger's syndrome

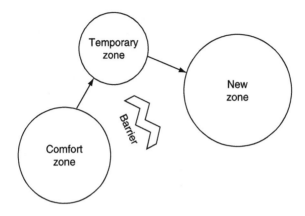

Bypass the barrier

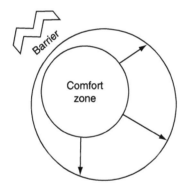

Accommodate the barrier

Figure 1.4 **Compensating for barriers**

and an isolated upbringing, give rise to a barrier to coaching on relationships and interpersonal skills. In this case, two things need to happen for Carl to be able to accept coaching in this area: first, he must acknowledge there is a problem and second, he must decide to do something about it. With the diagnosis of Asperger's syndrome it will lead to a compensation for Carl's difficulties with relationships, as shown in Figure 1.4, as it is unlikely he will ever be able to manage effective relationships well. With the alternative scenario of an isolated upbringing he needs to be taught the basic skills of relationships before being coached in how to use them. In this example the way forward would be to bypass the barrier to a temporary zone whilst he learnt new skills and practised these with the support of the coach alongside continuing to be coached in other areas as needed.

If the client's goals cannot be met with the barrier in place then the client may need to spend time with someone, a psychotherapist or counsellor for example, who is able to help the client dismantle the barrier and remove the block to progress.

The coach needs to be cautious and resist the temptation to push the client when faced with a barrier. It must be the client's choice, freely taken, on how to proceed. This can be thought of as similar to encouraging someone to jump from an aeroplane to take their first parachute descent and the coach who pushes them out of the door, however well meaning the intentions are. Just because the coach knows there is little or no risk involved does not take precedence over the client's right to choose what to do.

Traps

Once caught in a trap, no effective coaching can take place until the client has been able to release themselves, by their own efforts or with assistance. A trap is very similar to a barrier except that the client cannot move away until they are free. The key is an inability to move either forwards or backwards; retreating is not an option as it is when a client comes upon a barrier. A client caught in a trap is likely to be suffering, experiencing psychological pain, such that coaching has to stop until they are free from the trap and any wounds are healed.

Ghulam (Chapter 11) with his recurring problem of sexual identity is caught in a trap. He cannot continue with the coaching now that the issue of his homosexuality has become clear, nor can he retreat and carry on working on other areas. To benefit from coaching he must, first, find a way to release himself from the trap. Releasing himself does not necessarily mean dealing with the trap, or solving the psychological problems. This could come later if he chose. In this case, release from the trap would occur if he was able to accept that his homosexuality was not a work-related issue and he could then carry on focusing on other areas.

Frances (Chapter 10) is similarly trapped by her eating disorder. This is not an issue that is directly related to work, but has implications for the coaching direction. In neither of these two examples is the trap directly related to the coaching focus; it is an historical issue that comes out because the client is being coached.

One sign that suggests the client is trapped, psychologically, is the client who repeatedly agrees, and may even suggest, courses of action but does not carry them through. The client who becomes stuck may be caught in a trap.

A trap is likely to be related to the client's past, psychological baggage so to speak, where the act of coaching takes the client to the area where they are ensnared by these historical issues.

Turbulence

Turbulence is where something occurs that unbalances the client. This can be thought of as finding a patch of rough water on the journey, some psychological turbulence that may lead to the client either pushing ahead, with or without support, or retreating back to the safety of the comfort zone.

With this analogy, psychological turbulence is equivalent to an area of rough water on the journey and there can be two causes. The rough water may always be present in this place, which is analogous to passing through rapids on a river, or a tidal race at sea. Alternatively, the rough water may be due to the prevailing weather conditions – a storm approaching or the river may be very high due to torrential rain – and will pass; there may be smooth water in the same place tomorrow.

'Elizabeth's stressful life', described in Chapter 9, paints a picture of a woman who is leading a very turbulent life, she has too many pressures on her time to be able to cope and the stress this leads to causes concern. Elizabeth may have the personality that finds saying 'no' difficult, she may have a history of taking on too much, and exploring her background is very likely to lead to other examples of times in her life when she became highly stressed. Using the analogy of rough water, there are always rough areas for her, and the coach will need to help her to recognise them and avoid them whenever possible, as well as helping her to learn how to steer a safe course through the rapids.

Andrea (Chapter 5) is grieving; this is rough water that will pass in time. If the coach were able to start again in some months time, Andrea would probably find smooth water, the turbulence will have passed.

In the above two examples, the turbulence is all around; both Elizabeth and Andrea are experiencing rough water most of the time. There will be other cases where the rough water only occurs in certain places. This could be around a relationship or certain type of relationship for example. A generally successful male manager may find it impossible to be assertive with female team members (or vice versa) and find himself either giving in or getting very angry, but not able to address issues. Frances (Chapter 10), with her difficulties in being close to people, would be an example of this type of turbulence. The examples of rough water are endless, but thinking about it in these ways – is it permanently here, will it pass, can we navigate through it, can it be bypassed or compensated for? – may help with the decision making around what to do and if coaching is the best solution.

A final point to be considered with this idea that some clients may struggle with areas of turbulence is developing a dependence on the support of the coach to navigate through the rough water. A goal in coaching is to help the client to develop their own autonomy by learning strategies to use in the future. A client who is able to navigate through an area of psychological turbulence with the support of the coach, but who cannot learn from the experience, may become dependent on the coach and look for this support whenever there is a recurrence. Pointers to this occurring would include: emergency contact (the panic phone call for example), not carrying through on a plan, procrastinating about repeating some new behaviours without support from the coach and giving implausible reasons why coaching cannot end. The key is that the client is scared they cannot navigate rough water on their own.

The presence of psychological turbulence during coaching is likely to lead to the more difficult decisions. The signs will not be as clear as someone who is in a minefield (see below) or necessarily have an identifiable cause or trigger event as with a barrier or trap. The presence of turbulence will present challenges to the coach because the act of coaching may not always be a smooth journey and differentiating between what can be worked through and what needs some other form of help will not always be clear.

Minefields

A client in a minefield is beyond the scope of coaching and needs help from a mental health professional. This is the easiest of these types of problems to deal with, because the minefield is the province of the clear signs and symptoms discussed throughout this book where there is evidence of mental illness. Within the definitions being used here, a minefield will be a discomfort zone. Stop coaching and take appropriate action.

These analogies, of barriers, traps, turbulence and minefields help by painting a picture of the type of suffering the client may have. They build pictures that can be developed and extended in any ways that work, for example, 'has the mine exploded?' or 'are the mines on the surface (visible) or submerged (hidden, but detected in some way)?' 'Is the barrier made of bricks?' would indicate a solid, visible barrier, whereas a fog bank could indicate something impenetrable that may or may not contain something solid to hit. The usefulness is in the ability to generalise the behaviours shown by the client in a helpful way that aids the decision on what to do next.

Conclusion

Mental health is almost impossible to define; at best it will be an assumption with any client. Someone is assumed to be psychologically healthy until signs show otherwise. To judge behaviour as 'normal' relies on social context and the specific environment, and the person judging this brings in their own views.

At first glance the abnormal behaviours of mental illness may appear far easier to define, but this is only in the more extreme cases, and is an art, not a science. A picture can be built up by paying attention to certain groups of signs and then trying to classify these as a type of suffering rather than attempting a diagnosis.

The next chapter looks at how to recognise signs by developing an early warning system and then how to question in order to build up a more complete picture before deciding what to do.

Learning points

- Mental health is an assumption, not a fact.
- Signs of mental illness are all around.
- Watch out for:
  - ➤ changes
  - ➤ incongruity
  - ➤ attitudes
  - ➤ evasiveness.
- Is the suffering:
  - ➤ functional suffering
  - ➤ dysfunctional suffering
  - ➤ or mental illness?
- Is the issue impacting on the coaching? Is it:
  - ➤ a barrier
  - ➤ a trap
  - ➤ turbulence
  - ➤ a minefield?
- Can it be avoided or compensated for?

2

Gathering information

If the coach entered every session looking for signs and symptoms of some mental illness then it is quite likely they could be found. As outlined in Chapter 1, the signs of mental illness, psychological distress and psychosocial problems are all around. They form a part of normal behaviour for everyone.

It is the accumulation of signs, the impact on day-to-day behaviours, the severity and longevity that lead to concerns over the basic wellness of the client being raised.

If the ability to delay gratification is seen as a positive on an emotional intelligence scale and yet delaying gratification can be thought of as similar to depressing then, when does this positive behaviour flip over to a negative behaviour?

Think about a salesperson telephoning prospective clients day after day. Rationally they know that only a very small percentage of those calls will result in a sale and the emotional resilience to just keep going in a positive and upbeat way is vital to any success. This continual rejection will affect people in very different ways and, for some, it will prove too much. Just where this 'too much' point occurs is impossible to quantify – it will vary from person to person and from day to day.

What the coach needs is an early warning system that provides the ability to judge when normal behaviours that can be worked with in a positive and productive way are moving over to negative behaviours that need a different approach. This early warning system is always switched on, checks out the signs for authenticity and can respond in an appropriate way.

Warning bells

For warning bells to be effective, four parts to the system are needed:

- The bells must be in place.
- They need to be audible.
- There needs to be a system to decipher the message.
- And an ability to take appropriate action.

Building the bells

The most effective warning system is one that identifies the emergency at just the right time to take appropriate action. If the bells ring too often and with no easily identifiable cause then they will soon be ignored. Similarly, if the stimulus needed to ring the bells is very strong then it is harder to take action to avoid the emergency, the emergency will have happened before the coach is aware of it.

When coaching, the hope is that the client will be able to change. The goal is for the client to be able to move, psychologically, to a more productive way of being, to get more of what they want.

For the warning system to work, the first step is to recognise a need. Hopefully, the earlier chapters of this book will have shown how to identify that there is a need. The next task is to develop a range of bells that can be rung with different intensity, from a gentle 'ting', just an alert, to a full out 'claxon' that immediately leads to emergency action.

Developing the bells

Developing, or building, the warning bells has several components:

- Have an understanding of the enormous range of mental illness and psychosocial issues.

- Increase the knowledge of what can go wrong.
- Develop an awareness of the signs that clients may show.

Hearing the bells

During the coaching session the focus will be on the client and their agenda for change. The focus will not be looking, continually, for signs of mental illness; this would distract from the job of coaching. But, the sooner the warning bells can be heard then the sooner action can be taken to either change the focus or intensity of the coaching or take other action.

In Section 2 are a variety of client scenarios that will help develop an ear for the types of language and behaviours that may cause concern. In Section 3 are the symptoms that medical professionals are looking for when deciding on a diagnosis and the linking and accumulation of evidence that leads to a diagnostic decision and informs the choice of treatment.

Everyone has normal life experience to call on. Everyone will have their own views on what is appropriate and normal behaviour in a given situation. Many people will have some ideas as to what is abnormal psychological behaviour, gained from personal experience, dealing with a friend or family member who has had difficulties or from reading, watching television, etc.

This ability to recognise that something may be wrong is present in everyone, to some degree, all the time. Hearing the bells is about a way of paying attention whilst concentrating on something else.

Imagine enjoying a quiet evening in front of the television, relaxed, peaceful and paying attention to the programme. There will be an awareness, in the background, of noises other than the television. This could be a child upstairs in their bedroom, noises of cars outside on the street, your partner in the kitchen. You will be semiconsciously aware of them but able to ignore the noises and focus on the task, watching television. But, as soon as the noise becomes unusual you will take notice. You will also, probably, notice when an expected noise ceases. You will probably register that the loud music upstairs has been turned off; you may notice a car engine stopping outside. A noise stopping or an unusual noise occurring needs instant evaluation to decide whether to ignore it or take action.

This is hearing the bells, and without any training needed. The same system works around potential mental health issues. Without conscious thought or specific training, when a client starts to talk about their hallucinations, the fact that they are controlled by 'thought beams' from the office across the street or that they have no future and have saved up a bottle of sleeping pills to take tonight, no more training than life itself gives is needed to know that something is wrong. And the signs are so obvious that they will attract attention no matter where the focus is.

Thankfully, such clear and unequivocal signs of mental illness are extremely rare; the majority of coaches will never come across them in professional life. It is far more likely that something will occur that seems slightly unusual, but attracts attention. The coach needs to have their hearing tuned to notice these first hints that something may be unusual in the client's behaviour. The earliest signs may be the hardest to notice. Attention will be elsewhere and it may take some time for the signs to register. The client may need to show two, three or more discreet signs before your awareness triggers you to focus on them. Once attention has been drawn to something unusual it is quite likely that you will remember something from an earlier session that is additional information that has more relevance now.

The coach needs to be able to maintain a clear and active focus on the process and content of the session, whilst, at the same time, having the ability to become aware of warning signs that there may be something out of the ordinary going on for the client.

If the coach was able to have an observer present, with a brief to watch for signs, then the coach could concentrate on their job undisturbed. This is unlikely to happen; more commonly the coach will have the opportunity to discuss the coaching with a supervisor, or other consultative support, at a later date. One key task of the supervision process is to help the coach identify and take action when the client's behaviour suggests that coaching may not be the best course of action, but it is always retrospective. There may be a delay of some weeks between the client presenting with a difficult issue and the coach discussing this with their supervisor, and then a further delay until the next session with the client.

What the coach needs is an ability to invite an observer into the session to focus on the unusual and to alert the coach. A term borrowed from the counselling and psychotherapy field is 'internal supervisor', and Patrick Casement describes this as follows:

> They can thus learn to watch themselves as well as the patient, now using this island of intellectual contemplation as the mental space within which the internal supervisor can begin to operate. (Casement 1995: 32)

This means holding a part of one's attention to one side to watch the coaching that is in progress and has many uses, not just to alert the coach to potential mental health warning signs. It can be pictured, perhaps, by having a parrot sitting on your shoulder as you work. A parrot that is awake, alert and knowledgeable to draw attention to what is going on so that action can be taken. A parrot has been chosen because they are generally thought of as being intelligent and trainable. The coach's internal supervisor needs training and developing. Parrots can talk, but only what they have been taught to say. So, the more phrases the parrot has been taught the less likely is a generic alarm squawk. The parrot needs to learn to differentiate. Rather than just making a noise to attract attention it is more helpful if your parrot can say: 'Watch out, depression about!'

Teaching the parrot to talk is another way of saying, 'developing your internal supervisor' and means that the coach has to:

- Gain an understanding of mental illness.
- Recognise signs that might be seen whilst coaching.
- Reflect on sessions for anything unusual whilst making notes.
- Discuss cases with a supervisor/consultant or peers.

This will develop the ability to use the internal supervisor during sessions. The ideal is to move from a position where thought is needed to watch out for adverse signs to a place where intuition takes over, which means that the focus will be on coaching during the sessions but unusual behaviours will be recognised.

A clear and strong signal is easy to recognise. But, it is far more likely that small and subtle signs will occur that may need further exploration.

Deciphering the message

Whilst enjoying an interesting programme on television you hear a noise. Unless it is clear that immediate action is needed the most likely next step will be to wait to see if it is repeated, perhaps turning down the television volume to make it easier to hear. Part of your attention will be focused on the unexplained noise. If the noise is not repeated then your attention will turn back to the television programme. If the noise is repeated or there is another noise, then you will probably search for a reason.

Searching for a reason – was the noise the cat, a child, the wind? – can be an internal event whilst still paying attention to the programme. Or it may be active, leaving the television programme to check another room or outside, searching for a rational reason before deciding what, if any, action is needed.

Follow a similar process during coaching:

- A warning bell rings.
- Part of your attention focuses on this.
- If there is any substance in the warning then it is focused on either a passive (a listening watch) or an active (questioning) response.
- Look for an explanation.

The primary question to answer is: 'Is it safe and sensible to refocus on the coaching?' And, again, the easiest 'yes' or 'no' responses lie at the extremes. Far more likely is a 'yes, but', or 'no, but' answer:

- Yes, but, I'm going to watch out for a repeat.

- Yes, but, I will show more care in this area.
- Yes, but, I'm going to talk to my supervisor.
- No, but, I need more information.

The coach will not be making a decision based on one piece of evidence, except in rare and extreme cases. The accumulation of evidence based on several separate, but linked, pieces of information leads to a change in the coaching due to mental health reasons. When the coach has started to pay active attention to the warning bells they may realise, with hindsight, that there were signs in earlier sessions or in information about the client from other sources. The coach needs to build up a more complete picture by putting all the pieces together. Once the coach has identified a potential issue and started to collect evidence, then each piece of information can be stored in the corner of their mind to be called upon as needed.

What is being searched for is a clear-enough picture for the coach to be able to choose an appropriate course of action. The picture does not have to be precise or complete in every detail, it need only be clear enough to guide the coach towards a choice of how to proceed. Whilst building up a picture, score the items that are being 'stored in the corner'. Does this piece of evidence add to or subtract from suspicions? Is it primary evidence or supportive?

Such a logical process may seem difficult or unnatural during the session itself. If the normal style of coaching face to face involves taking notes then jot down concerns, similarly, make notes during telephone coaching. If taking notes during the session is inappropriate then spend some time reviewing and writing down the details as soon as possible after the session. In those cases that do not suggest a clear course of action during the session then a clear and complete set of notes acts as a reminder for reflecting upon before the next session and in discussions with a supervisor or consultant. Notes may become vital should the client's problems escalate and the professional behaviour of the coach comes under scrutiny (see Chapter 3).

Three areas in particular should be questioned once attention is focusing on unusual behaviours. Summed up in the PPP (Past, Pervasive, Plan) system of questioning (Table 2.1), the three areas that need attention are the history of the unusual behaviour, how much of the client's life is affected and whether they have a plan of how to deal with it.

Past

Questions such as, 'How long have you felt like this?' help to contextualise the client's behaviour in the session. There is a significant difference between someone feeling hopeless and depressed today and someone who has felt like this for several months, but who, maybe, has just not talked about it before.

Similarly, 'Has this happened before?' will help to build a picture and choose a suitable course of action. Repeating patterns of behaviour can be important indicators of mental illness and psychosocial stress. Repeating patterns may also lead to a resolution that the client can pick up on. If the client is able to identify similarities between 'now' and 'then' they may be able to remember how they dealt with these issues before and, if that was successful, repeat the same plan.

It may well be that the client is unaware that warning bells have been ringing. They may feel that they are behaving perfectly normally and rationally, but the coach has concerns. For example, a client repeatedly pushes away personal

Table 2.1 **The PPP system of questioning**

Past	What is the history of this behaviour or feeling? For how long has the client had similar feelings? Has this happened before?
Pervasive	How much of the client's life is involved? Is this a home issue that has crossed over to work today? Is it a work issue that is impacting on home life? Or are all parts of the client's life affected?
Plan	Does the client have a plan? Is the plan positive? Is the plan realistic, will it work? Will the plan be carried out, is there commitment?

responsibility. This may be blaming others, or, being seemingly stuck in a 'there's nothing I can do about that' powerless position. If the response to a straight forward question such as, 'If you can't do anything about this issue, what can you do something about?' does not allay concerns then try to find out if it is recent, at work, or part of a longer-term inability to accept personal responsibility.

Pervasive

A work issue, a home issue or a whole of life issue?

If a client is feeling anxious and unsupported ask: 'Who does support you?' or 'Where do you feel supported?' The answer that there is lots of support through family and friends, just not at work, can be seen to be different to: 'No one supports me, no one can help.'

There are circumstances where a seemingly work-related issue that has caused concern may need clarifying. Questioning around other parts of the client's life can help build up a clearer picture.

For example a female client appears to be very distressed in the session. She is upset about the behaviour of a male colleague and how this has affected her. Questions such as, 'Has this happened before?' and 'Who with?' can help unravel what is going on. This may be a straightforward issue of workplace bullying, sexual harassment or similar, which, however distressing, can be dealt with. Alternatively the client may have experienced sexual abuse many years ago and an incident at work has brought this back to her.

Questioning about the client's past and the pervasiveness of feelings and behaviours may reduce or remove the coach's concerns about the client's behaviour. The client may be able to stop the warning bells from ringing by answering clearly and rationally and give a 'yes' to the question, 'Is it safe and sensible to refocus on the coaching?'

Plan

Does the client have a plan of what to do?

A plan of what to do about the issues that have arisen is

a very positive step. For the client to start to work on a plan of action there first needs to be recognition that something is wrong.

It does not necessarily follow that just because the coach's warning bells have been ringing and the 'story' has been checked out, the client will be in agreement that there is a potential psychological or psychosocial issue that needs attention. If there is an issue that suggests a course of action other than coaching and the client disagrees then the coach is faced with making a decision for both parties (this is explored further in Chapters 3 and 4), but with or without client acceptance of the warning bells, exploration of plans will be beneficial.

In cases where the coach has concerns and the client does not agree then a plan of action will 'buy' some time in all but the most extreme cases and the coach can hold a listening watch in future sessions for a recurrence of the issues. The client may not need to actively agree with the coach's view of things for them to have taken on board what has been said. With the stigma that is attached to mental health issues, some people may struggle to go along with the coach's view at first. The client is the 'expert' on themselves and another possibility is that the coach has misread the situation completely.

Whichever of these three possibilities proves to be the closest, with hindsight, questioning around and discussion of a plan will be helpful for both the coach and client.

The best predictor for change (whether recovery from a mental illness or resolution of a psychosocial issue) is recognition of the problem and a plan to do something about it.

When listening to a plan in these types of circumstance, follow the process in the same way as helping a client make a plan to change behaviour in more normal circumstances. Is the plan reasonable? Is it likely to work and meet the client's needs? How committed is the client to the plan?

A sensible-sounding plan that is in the client's powers to carry through will probably reduce the level of warning bells ringing. It may be appropriate to continue coaching if the client has a plan to visit their doctor, for example, or to discuss matters with their line manager or human resources department. Whereas without a firm intent on the part of the client to do something the coach may decide that coaching should stop.

There are plans that will escalate the degree of concern and the response by the coach. The client may show a high degree of commitment to a detailed plan that is destructive to themself or another person or property. It goes without saying that a well-formed plan to commit suicide or to deliberately self-harm will not be seen as a positive sign. Similarly, for example, a client showing signs of borderline personality disorder and paranoia may form a plan to defend themself by sabotaging a company or another person.

Plans that cannot be easily checked should be viewed with a degree of suspicion. For example, concerns may have been raised about the use/abuse of alcohol or recreational drugs and the client says that they recognise this has become an issue and will stop or cut down. The coach may be the first person who has openly asked about an issue such as this and the client's first response may be to 'hide the evidence' and try to pretend there is not a problem. Pretending to accept the coach's view and agreeing to change, but with no real intention to follow through, is particularly common with an addictive behaviour.

A plan may contribute to a prediction of positive change but a plan alone does not mean that everything is all right. The plan needs to lead to a change in behaviour or feelings before the coach can return to working as normal.

After the first sound of warning bells the coach will be passively listening for more information or actively questioning to help build up a picture. The questioning is a balancing act between finding out information and maintaining the relationship with the client. If after one or two warning signs the coach stops coaching and starts interrogating the client the relationship that has been built up is likely to be irretrievably damaged. It is important that, whenever possible, the coach maintains a good relationship with their client. The foundations of this are trust and respect, and these need to be maintained so that the coaching can reach a satisfactory conclusion for both parties, even if the conclusion is ending the coaching prematurely.

Once warning bells have been heard and the coach is assessing these for validity, great care should be taken not to slip into a 'helping the client' way of working. Should it be decided that the coach is the person best placed to help the client with the particular issue, the helping process starts in the future. At this stage the coach is assessing the client, exploring issues, trying to get as full a picture as possible as to what is going on for the client. The coach should not be tempted to start counselling or offering practical suggestions.

The case of Brian in Chapter 6 shows how this change of roles for the coach could happen. Brian says: '... it just seems so meaningless now'; for the coach to respond with 'What's meaningless?' is reasonable, except that the coach is focusing on when things started to go wrong for Brian in a work-based setting and asks: 'When did it become meaningless?', a question that asks for factual information on the past. This leads to a trigger event becoming clear. Explore the whole picture to get information to answer the question, 'What is best for the coaching?' before focusing on a specific area. In this example the question that needs answering is something like the golf coach and frozen shoulder issue from the Introduction, where the golf coach does not need to know anything more about the shoulder than it is painful and restricting movement. Brian has pain and is restricted in his ability to engage in the coaching; the coach needs to know what, if any, barrier to coaching this pain will prove to be rather than what the pain is.

This is an area that those coaches who have come from a therapeutic or counselling background may need to be particularly careful around. Internal supervision is the check on straying into therapy or counselling inappropriately; listen to your parrot.

After the session

An effective warning system and a way to check out the validity of the signs is the first step in the process leading to a decision on the most appropriate route forward. There may be instances where a decision needs to be made immediately or where an appropriate way forward seems clear, the decision being relatively straightforward. Probably more likely is the situation where the coach thinks that something needs to be done, but is not yet ready to take action. After an unusual session it is important to take the time to reflect back on what happened. Note taking is an important part of this. Make clear, detailed process notes. A record of what actually happened could be important for future records; it will be helpful to the coach to refer to before the next contact with the client. Make notes about thoughts and feelings as the session developed as well as thoughts and feelings whilst reflecting on the session later.

After something puzzling or unusual has happened with a client, having a consultative arrangement with an experienced professional is very helpful. The supervisor, mentor, coach, consultant or manager who is on hand to explore with the coach the process of the coaching session, what triggered the warning bells and talk through the options serves several purposes. There is a formal opportunity to talk over what may have been happening; this will help clarify the thoughts of the coach. There is an opportunity to get someone else's view, someone who is slightly removed from the actuality of the session to check out the reality of the coach's suspicions. Often the supervisory relationship will be with someone more experienced, someone who can bring a different dimension or viewpoint to the coaching and be able to look at other interpretations. The supervisor will help with discussions of the best approach, helping take into account any ethical issues, such as client confidentiality, and may have practical advice to offer.

One important point that the supervisor can cover is to double check that the coach has not confused 'my stuff' with 'your stuff'. This is a sense check that the coach has not been misinterpreting the signs by making an assumption based on something from the coach's past or that the client has not triggered a response by 'pushing the coach's buttons'. If a client starts to talk in a way that reminds the coach of an historical event, which could be a challenging client from the past or something personal, there is the possibility that the interpretation the coach makes could be biased towards what happened before or even that the coach could subconsciously try to 'take care of' this client because they could not 'take care of' the other person. The supervisor is there to check that the coach is reacting in the reality of the situation and taking action that is appropriate to the situation.

Gathering information is a vital part of the decision-making process and, unless immediate emergency action is needed, should be detailed and thorough. The focus is on the ability of the client to gain advantage from being coached, not on any diagnosis. Following a system of questioning reduces the chance of missing an important clue that could either increase or decrease the risks of continuing with the coaching.

Learning points

- The goal is to decide if coaching can continue, not to diagnose mental illness.
- Develop an early warning system – the warning bells.
- Listen to the parrot.
- After hearing the warning bells, explore further.
- Question using PPP:
  ➢ past
  ➢ pervasive
  ➢ plan.
- Discuss suspicions of mental health problems with a consultant or supervisor.
- Make notes.

3

Considerations

In the dictionary 'consideration' is defined as both a fact to be taken into account when making a decision and careful thought. This chapter explores a host of legal, ethical, moral and practical considerations that may impact on the decision-making process whilst progressing along the line to finding an answer to the question 'should coaching continue?', and if coaching is to continue has the substance and structure been changed and if coaching is thought to be inappropriate what needs consideration as part of ending the relationship? Chapter 4 looks in greater detail at the choices faced by the coach from continuing to coach, through coaching alongside other support, to ending the relationship, perhaps by initiating other professional contact, and highlights the specific issues likely to need thought with each choice (see Table 4.1, p. 76).

Identification of a psychological issue is the first piece of the jigsaw that leads to an end picture of how the coaching relationship might look. The goal is a clear picture that holds together when viewed from different angles. These angles include the coach's viewpoint, that of the client, any third party involved, any appropriate professional standards, associated indemnity insurance providers, a legal viewpoint and from society as a whole (Figure 3.1). Does the final decision on how to proceed hold good when viewed from each of these perspectives?

Every case is unique, every client different, every coach distinct and in each case the merits of one course of action over another need consideration to allow for some clarity in

Figure 3.1 **The plan needs looking at from every angle**

the choices available. This chapter is more a list of questions to consider than a 'what to do when — happens'. Thinking in advance about a variety of potential issues will make it more likely that a wise course of action will be chosen when the need arises with a client. The questions are divided into three main areas (Table 3.1): the coaching context, coaching delivery and the likely efficacy (will the coaching produce the intended results). Some of the questions have more relevance at one end of the scale of options than the other. For example, the coach's ability to avoid working therapeutically with a client has little relevance if coaching is stopped and confidentiality is not an issue unless another party needs to become involved.

Those coaches who are members of one of the coaching associations will have the help and guidance provided by a statement of ethics, good practice and professional standards, where boundaries are set of what is and is not considered appropriate behaviour. These are routinely available via the internet (see the References for a selection). Those in other professions and positions may have similar guidelines to help them.

Table 3.1 **Considerations**

The coaching context
- The contract?
- Confidentiality issues?
- Where is it happening?
- At work?
- Privately?
- Who is paying?

The coaching delivery
- Face to face?
- On the telephone?
- A combination?
- Frequency?
- Duration?

The coaching efficacy
- Will coaching produce the intended results?
- For the client?
- Any third party?
- The coach?
- From a professional standards viewpoint?
- Within the competencies of the coach?

What follows starts from the point in time when a coach has come to the conclusion, with or without the client's agreement, that there is evidence of a psychological, psychosocial or mental health issue. In some cases there will be time to think through a course of action, to take advice from others, maybe to do some research, at the very least time to reflect on what may have been going on. In other situations an immediate response may be necessary. Unfortunately, those times when the right choice is most important are the ones when the decision needs taking promptly. At the extreme, as an example, a telephone-coaching client has been becoming increasingly low and fed up, in this session his voice is slurred and he says: 'What's the point, it's time to say goodbye', then hangs up. The coach does not have the time to reflect on this or to speak to a supervisor but needs to make a decision immediately; to telephone the emergency services or not? This client may be intending to commit suicide, alternatively they may have had a couple of drinks at lunchtime, which has bolstered their courage enough to say they no longer want any coaching, a subject they have been trying to raise for the last three sessions. What would you do?

The coaching context

The context in which the coaching is taking place has a variety of issues that need considering by the coach in order to help them choose the best way forward (Table 3.1).

The contract

As soon as a prospective client makes contact with a coach a contract is in place. There is the expectation of certain standards of behaviour, such as confidentiality, that make up the expected professionalism of the coach. Irrespective of any formal, written agreement that may follow, there is an immediate presumption of a contract based on the expected nature of the coach – client relationship. Someone using the term 'coach' or 'coaching' to attract a client will be expected to adhere to the normal standards presumed locally irrespective of any formal training, associated memberships, indemnity insurance, etc. 'I never offered confidentiality' is likely to be viewed as a poor defence should a client take a coach to court for misconduct. This contract forms the basis of the rules governing how the coach behaves, what is being offered and the expectations of what will follow. A formal contract may follow detailing specifics such as times, fees, responsibilities and covering limits to confidentiality. The contract may be different when a third party is paying compared to the client paying directly; the coach must balance the needs of both the client and the sponsoring organisation.

Confidentiality

One of the cornerstones of any coaching relationship and formal or informal contract is the privacy and confidentiality of the arrangement and the information that is held in trust within the relationship. To break confidentiality, to disclose confidential information or to share a judgement with another person based on the client's behaviour needs careful consideration.

The most acceptable way to break confidentiality is with the client's informed consent. Informed consent means that the coach has made the effort to help the client understand the likely consequences of breaking confidentiality. Has the client given consent to speak to one specific person or agency, or is the client comfortable that the coach will manage discussions with others appropriately? For example a client may give permission for the coach to speak to the human resources director but not their line manager (or vice versa), their sister but not their brother-in-law. But, what to do when the brother-in-law answers the telephone and the sister is unavailable for three days?

Should the coach judge it to be necessary to break confidentiality without the express permission of the client then care needs taking, in advance, to think through the likely consequences. Whenever possible the client needs to be informed in advance that the coach will be communicating with others, be told who the coach will be speaking to and what information will be shared.

There are instances when the coach must break confidentiality rules, with or without any client consent. There are circumstances where the law will demand that the coach approaches others with confidential material. Areas covered by a legal obligation to break confidentiality include, but not exclusively, issues such as child protection, prevention of terrorism (sometimes covered by a catch-all phrase such as 'in the best interest of society') and where there is a threat of serious bodily harm to self or others. These categories can be viewed as top-level exceptions and override any other specific defences and obligations that may be in place in the circumstances. These are the permissions and obligations to break confidentiality from the viewpoint of society and the law.

There may be other times when the coach must consider breaking confidentiality without the client's permission when a contract exists with a third party. Most commonly this will be as part of business or executive coaching when a sponsoring organisation is providing and paying for coaching for an employee. The coach may be obliged under the terms of the contract to comment on the ability of the client to benefit from coaching, there could be a clause about harming the company, by intent or otherwise, or bringing the company into disrepute. The terms of the contract in business coaching may lead to some difficult decisions for the coach when the client is showing signs of mental illness, a conflict between what is best for the client and what is best for the company could arise.

The intent of the law of breaking confidentiality is around bodily harm, a danger of suicide or concern that the client will physically harm another. With a third-party contract the clause is most likely to be quite vague and around harming the organisation in general. A potential conflict for the coach could be when something comes to light that may jeopardise the company financially or otherwise. For example a coach is working with the finance director (FD) of a publicly quoted company who talks of cutting corners in the annual accounts, they may be depressed and just cannot be bothered, or even hallucinating that they have received instructions to follow a certain course of action. What is best for the client, best for the company and best for the coach are different in this example. The client will need help to return to normal functioning, the company needs to know that its probity and future are not compromised and the coach has to balance a duty of care to the client with fulfilling contractual obligations to the company, whilst keeping to professional standards. Following this example, the FD does not agree with the coach's view that there is anything wrong and says, 'no one ever checks the accounts anyway' and then quite angrily ends coaching, finishing with a vague threat should the coach tell anyone. After reflection and discussion with the coach's supervisor, several points arise:

- Is the FD likely to continue the damaging course of action?
- How likely does the coach think it that the FD will seek help for his problems?

- Should the coach choose to do nothing, is their professional standing jeopardised?
- Should the coach choose to do nothing, is there a breach of the contract with the company?
- If the coach decides to breach confidentiality, what are the likely consequences, professionally and personally?
- What is the correct route to breaching confidentiality, who to tell and how? If the normal point of contact is with someone junior to the FD (human resources or training manager for example), is a telephone conversation sufficient to fulfil any obligations, or should the coach approach someone higher in the organisation's structure?
- How far should the coach go in making sure that the company takes appropriate action to avoid any damage the FD may cause?

On the issue of breaking client confidentiality there can be seen to be an approximate order of precedent to follow. First are the laws currently in force, then obligations under any specific contract. Make appropriate choices under these and the result is likely to be viewed favourably by an indemnity insurance provider and any professional body that the coach subscribes to, which form the next tier of responsibility, followed by the wishes and moral views of the client and coach.

The indemnity insurance provider is the safety net should a client decide to sue the coach for misconduct. Most have a legal help desk to offer advice on issues that may be helpfully used as part of the process of deciding to break client confidentiality. Looking at the issue from this angle will include both strict legal views and how the coach has behaved in view of any codes of ethics and good practice. These codes of ethics provided by coaching organisations, and agreed to by the membership of that organisation, provide a general view of what is considered good practice at a professional level. They are there to help the coach behave within the norms of professional life and, whilst not necessarily legally binding, the organisation can censure the coach with specific training or other requirements or expel them from the membership.

On this subject of breaking client confidentiality, there seems to be general agreement that coaches maintain confidentiality except when doing so would break the law.

The code of ethics of the International Association of Coaches (IAC) states: 'Unless prohibited by law, coaches will only disclose confidential information if the client, or person legally authorized to consent on behalf of the client, has given express written consent' (IAC, 2003: 4.04a) and 'Coaches may disclose confidential information without the consent of the client only as mandated or permitted by law' (IAC 2003: 4.04b). The International Coach Federation (ICF) asks member coaches to agree to the statement: 'I will respect the confidentiality of my client's information, except as otherwise authorized by my client, or as required by law' (ICF 2005: clause 22). The Association for Coaching (AC) includes confidentiality in a similar fashion and expects its member coaches to keep themselves informed of any statutory or legal requirements that may affect their work (AC 2005: clause 8).

The statement of standards and ethics of the European Coaching Institute (ECI) has paragraphs on breaking confidentiality where the coach believes there is compelling evidence of serious danger to the client or others and also that 'Coaches will operate within applicable laws, rules and regulations and will not, assist, persuade or collude with others engaged in conduct which is dishonest, unprofessional, unlawful or discriminatory in any way' (ECI 2005: B v & vi). The IAC has an addition to disclosure beyond harm to self or others, saying: 'Coaches must disclose certain confidential information as required by law or if the confidential information may put the client or others at risk of harm or compromise their wellbeing' (IAC 2005: 4.04e).

The code of ethics of the IAC and the statement of standards and ethics of the ECI bring in some potential dilemmas for the coach in these two points (above). With the example of the FD outlined above, where would the coach stand on breaking confidentiality if the contract did not involve a third party, if this was a private arrangement paid for by the FD? It may be that there is no legal case to answer for keeping the information confidential as no one is likely to be physically harmed by the actions of the FD in his poor accounting, but his actions are unprofessional, possibly dishonest under the terms of the ECI statement of standards and ethics and could compromise the wellbeing of others under the terms of the IAC code of ethics. Would the coach who did not disclose the FD's likely actions receive censure if the company was investigated for malpractice or went bankrupt and their prior knowledge became public?

How will a decision to break client confidentiality be viewed by the client and the coach? In a paradoxical way the views of the two people most affected by any decision to breach confidentiality are the last views to consider. If private, potentially damaging, information is shared with others it is the client's life that will be most affected and it is the coach who, ultimately, makes the decision. The laws, contractual obligations and guidelines provided by statements of ethics are a 'stick' to both force the coach to take this step and to help the coach with any later feelings, such as guilt, by allowing the coach to believe their actions were right within the law or obligatory under a contract. The final decision-making variables within this process are the moral codes, values and beliefs that the coach operates under. How comfortable will the coach be with any decision taken when the event is looked back on in later life?

No professional is likely to take a decision to disclose confidential material without consent unless absolutely necessary; far more likely will be discussions with the client on the value and necessity of disclosure that leads to an acceptable compromise. Some of these compromises are discussed in Chapter 4 and in Section 2, in Andrea's story (Chapter 5) for example.

Effectively, the coach that chooses to break confidentiality has taken control of aspects of the client's life and future and stepped well beyond the boundaries of any coaching relationship. But, in the context of this subject, the client will be experiencing some form of psychological distress to the extent that they may be likely to take actions that they would not normally consider. The coach may well be about to cause some immediate problems that are far less severe than the likely consequences of the client continuing unchecked.

When the decision has been taken to break client confidentiality, with or without the client's permission, the goal is twofold: to take steps to ensure the future wellbeing of the client and to limit any potential damage the client may cause to others. In some cases, communicating the information to one person may fulfil both goals, in others the coach may need to speak to more than one person.

Give the minimum information necessary to follow the client's wishes or fulfil the duty of care for the coaching client. Do not gossip, do not make a diagnosis, take care to stick to the facts in a professional way. It is possible that the coach may feel unduly uncomfortable talking about confidential issues and feel the need to gain agreement that talking to someone else was the right thing to do. Seeking approval could lead to excessive justification, giving unnecessary information and engaging in a judgemental conversation with someone else, even sharing stories about the issues the client has raised. Most people will view the coach as a professional, with the expertise to know that the course of action being suggested is a good choice.

To move things forward for the client without disclosing more information than is necessary, phrases such as:

'In my view the client would be best served by seeing a mental health professional.'

'The client has raised issues that suggest something other than coaching would be best at the moment.'

'I'm not sure how beneficial coaching would be at the moment, I've suggested a visit to the doctor as the first step.'

'I'm really concerned for this client's wellbeing, I think they must be seen by a doctor promptly.' Or even, 'We need to contact the emergency services.'

The goal is to discharge any responsibility in a professional manner, passing on to a more appropriate person the future care for the client. Take care not to take on responsibility for the client in matters that fall outside the coaching contract.

With the example of the FD (above), when the concern is

that he may damage the company, something like, 'I have real concerns over his ability to handle his job at the moment, I think he may do something he will regret in the future. Who do I need to speak to to help him get the support he needs at work and, probably, medically?' will meet the needs of all rather than talking about unprofessional behaviour, cutting corners, depression or not completing the accounts properly.

Pass on the minimum information needed to reach the goal.

Setting

The coaching setting is the physical environment in which coaching takes place. This could be personal or life coaching in the coach's home office or consulting room elsewhere; private coaching by telephone; business or executive coaching at a place of work, in the coach's office or other place, or on the telephone. The setting in which coaching takes place affects the choices open to the coach when a client starts to behave unusually. The setting brings in questions about how cautious the coach may wish to be.

Telephone coaching lacks all the physical clues that are visible face to face and the coach may choose to take a more cautious approach in continuing. Many of the signs of mental illness are physical, personal care and body language are important for example. Not being in a position to have these aids as part of the coaching suggests a more cautious approach both in evaluating issues and in continuing any coaching contact.

A life coach working from a home office is more exposed to possible problems than an executive coach who visits a client in his or her office at work. One obvious possibility is the disturbed client who becomes angry, abusive or violent and how exposed the coach could be in these circumstances. Another possibility is the client who cannot maintain contact boundaries and starts to visit the coach at unscheduled times or continue to make contact after coaching has been formally ended.

The setting suggests to the coach how rigorous they should be in sticking to the original coaching goals or reason for the client to ask for coaching. Whilst there may be clear cases where it is to the client's advantage to maintain coaching through a period of functional suffering, the case needs viewing within the context of the coaching. For the life or personal coach working with a client privately a clear discussion on what is likely to be achieved in the short term can be the forerunner to an agreement to keep going, with the knowledge that there may be some wasted time, from a coaching perspective, and progress may be slower than expected. With executive or business coaching the likely view of the sponsoring company needs to be taken into account, not just the views of the coach and client.

A client's father unexpectedly dies. In their own unique way the client will go through a period of grieving the loss, anything from a period when functioning is severely impaired to giving the appearance of continuing with no change. But the coach notices a lowering of mood, a loss of vitality, maybe a lack of focus. There is no suggestion that the client needs any other support than that provided by friends and family but the coaching will be affected whilst the client goes through a period of readjustment. The life coach could provide an anchor to normality in a case like this, a reminder that life will return to normal can be provided by the action of coaching, continuing to work on goals that fulfil the client's future aspirations; at a slower pace perhaps, with some thought around how the client is feeling on this particular day and with care that coaching is taking place rather than counselling or therapy, but still meeting the client's needs in a professional manner. For the executive coach, and without any reference to training and experience, it could be the same coach; the decision may well be different. What would be the views of the company on the coach giving time to the manager who is coming to terms with a loss and unable to take advantage of the coaching opportunity? How would others view the expense of several wasted hours of coaching? How will the coach's professional expertise be viewed if the expected results are not met? With executive coaching and third party involvement a break in coaching may be indicated.

Payment of fees

Coaching is normally a professional engagement and involves payment. As indicated above, who is paying is a consideration in the decision on whether to continue coaching or not. A coaching agreement or contract will involve fees and the client or other is paying for coaching with the expectation that there will be results. One of the considerations as to ending a coaching agreement is raised by the question: is coaching happening? If coaching is not happening due to a psychological barrier, what justification has the coach for continuing to charge? The key here is the word 'coaching'. There may be times when a continuing relationship may be theoretically beneficial but coaching cannot take place. Is the client emotionally able to have a coaching conversation?

Fees can have an impact in a variety of ways. There may be newly qualified coaches, working hard to build up a business but struggling to find clients, when letting a potential fee pass is a difficult decision. 'What harm am I doing when I continue to coach this grieving client when the company is paying anyway?' could be one thought linked to the example above when a break in coaching may be the best option. The client is not able to take part in the coaching, perhaps due to depression, a personality disorder or other issue, but says they want to continue anyway. However much a part of coaching having an optimistic outlook is, when will the coach stop taking fees if the client is unlikely to benefit?

Many coaches have a strong psychotherapy or counselling background and have the ability and experience to deal with psychological issues very competently. This type of coach faces the decision to refer to someone else and lose the fees of a client they may well be able to help in a different setting. In a business context the coach has been engaged, presumably, to coach a person in business-related skills and the line between coaching and therapy can be much clearer than with the life or personal coach. The question to ask is: 'Am I coaching this client, or engaging in therapy?' If the latter then the coach must discuss this with the client and work towards a solution. Clients may well have no knowledge of there being a difference; the duty lies with the coach to open the conversation.

In an ideal world the potential loss of fees would play no part in any coaching decision. In the real world, taking on a borderline client, one who would possibly benefit from therapy more than coaching, or continuing to coach the client with psychological issues are questions that many coaches will face.

The coaching delivery

How the coaching is delivered in a practical sense needs consideration as part of the decision-making process. The lack of visible clues as to what is going on has already been mentioned in relation to telephone coaching.

Questions to consider are the mode of delivery: face to face, telephone and e-mail perhaps. Where this is happening: private and safe, private but possibly exposed (for the coach and client), semi-public, such as the client's office, public, such as a seating area in a hotel. And how often. Is the contact structured and regular, infrequent, flexible? If the coaching plan is for infrequent formal contact, is support available between sessions, by telephone or e-mail? Is this support left for the client to ask for, or will the coach contact the client?

The decision to continue or stop the coaching due to the practicalities of delivery is not, necessarily, straightforward. It does not follow that regular face-to-face coaching is more beneficial than infrequent telephone contact. A question to ask is: 'How will the method of delivery benefit this client?'

Considerations include the client's ability to cope with the length of session, are they emotionally strong enough to work for an hour or longer? Would shorter contact be better?

Is the client's ability to join in the coaching variable? If the session needs arranging well in advance, how likely is it that the client will be OK at the specified time. Would a more flexible arrangement be beneficial?

Does the coach need the clues offered visually to be able to judge 'where the client is' today, or to be sure that the client is not becoming worse? If so, is telephone coaching appropriate?

How task oriented is the coaching? Do the frequency and quantity of tasks or homework assignments benefit the client? For some, clear, maybe substantial tasks, with a good length of time to complete them will be beneficial as the client can pick and choose when to work on them, depending on how they are feeling. For others, frequent, small, tasks may be best, as the client will be reminded as they go along and not get overwhelmed by the amount to do.

Is the frequency of the coaching appropriate? Does the frequency benefit the client? Is little and often likely to be more beneficial than fewer, longer sessions or vice versa? Does the coaching frequency impact on the client seeing someone else, a therapist for example?

Is the duration of the coaching of any benefit to the client? If the contract is for a brief period, for example three months, is this likely to be of benefit if the client is in a psychologically difficult place? Knowing what is going on for the client, emotionally, does the duration of the coaching offer any expectation of meeting their original goals in seeking coaching?

When all of the above, the method, frequency and the duration of delivery, are considered as a whole, does the proposed coaching seem ethically, morally and practically sound when viewed from all angles (see Figure 3.1)? Taking the opportunity to discuss the proposal with a consultant or supervisor will help the coach to think through the likely consequences of the coaching and highlight any unhelpful consequences.

The coaching efficacy

The efficacy of the coaching is about producing the intended result. A consideration as part of the decision-making process is the likelihood of the coaching being beneficial and in line with the original stated aims and the contract. A client may need help and support, the coach may be a competent person to offer this, but help and support is not coaching and the appropriate decision may be to stop. The likely effectiveness of coaching a client with a psychological issue needs to be considered from all the views illustrated in Figure 3.1 to check out, in advance, whether the agreed benefits seem to be reasonably achievable. The decision on how to proceed is not simply a case of the coach and client agreeing that they will continue.

A very important question to ask is whether the substance of any continued relationship between the coach and client can be termed 'coaching'. Consider this from the professional standards and indemnity insurance perspective, should something go wrong and the client take action against the coach then the substance of the relationship, what went on during conversations, will come into question. If the coach subscribes to one of the coaching organisation codes of ethics and best practice and has indemnity insurance, these will cover the practice of coaching and not any other form of relationship. For example, should the substance of the relationship be best termed 'therapy' or 'counselling' then, irrespective of the training and competency of the coach, indemnity insurance that specifies the activity 'coaching' will not cover these other types of relationship. This may be relevant to the experienced therapist who has changed their career to retrain and embrace coaching who may find problems with both a professional body and insurance provider should a client complain of malpractice. Similarly, a coach who is providing emotional support to a client may be in breach of contract with an organisation that thinks they have paid for coaching for an executive.

If coaching, as an activity, cannot be reasonably expected to produce the intended results then any continuing relationship with a client experiencing mental health, psychological or psychosocial issues should be approached with caution. Experience and appropriate training may allow some coaches to continue with a client when less experienced colleagues may choose to stop.

The principle of 'do no harm' or 'do the least harm', known as non-maleficence, is best placed near the top of the coach's thoughts when considering whether to continue or not with a client showing signs that may prove a barrier to coaching. A potential issue that may arise is when the client has self-selected coaching as a way to deal with their problems because of the different perception that coaching has over counselling or psychotherapy – the client feels that it is acceptable to have a personal or life coach, but may struggle to seek help from a counsellor. An employer may choose to offer coaching to a struggling employee as a more palatable option than suggesting a visit to the doctor or other mental health professional. In both these cases it will be the judgement of the coach who recognises the signs and symptoms of mental health issues that offers the best hope for the client in finding the most appropriate route to help. The coach who continues once signs of problems have become evident risks harming the client, delaying the client finding other forms of help or decreasing any motivation on the part of the client to seek professional advice for their problems in the future.

If a client approaches a coach looking for benefits that are unlikely to be achieved due to a psychological barrier, such as an historic unresolved issue, and the coach does not feel confident that they can answer 'yes' to the question 'Can coaching help this person?' then referral is the best option. The question is: 'Can coaching help?' not 'Can I help?' This may sound a pedantic point, but it is important in the context of the ethics of decision making. For the coach with a therapeutic background, asking this question helps to avoid slipping from coaching to counselling inadvertently and for the non-therapeutic coach it is a safeguard against unintentionally trying to work with a client who would be best served by some other form of help.

If no clear benefit seems obvious from coaching someone who has shown signs of emotional disturbance, however temporary these may appear to be, then do not coach.

Learning points

Considerations before making a plan:
- The contract.
- Who is paying?
- Method of delivery.
- Will coaching work?

Does the plan work for:
- The client.
- The coach.
- The employer or organisation paying?

Have the implications been considered from:
- The client's view.
- The coach's perspective.
- A professional standards or coaching ethics statement.
- An indemnity insurance provider's view.
- A legal perspective?

4

What next?

No matter how skilled at accurately identifying signs of mental illness they are, the coach will fail, professionally, without the ability to choose the most appropriate way forward.

'What next' is the most important of all the segments that make up the process of dealing with mental health issues in a professional relationship.

'What next' is the behaviour that is visible and will be the point on which the coach will be judged by the client, any third party and the world at large. An ill-chosen course of action at this stage could lead to problems for the client, the coach and any third party. Both ignoring the signs and taking excessive action could lead to professional censure, maybe a claim for malpractice being laid, as well as increasing the problems for the client.

For the client, ignoring the signs could lead to an escalation of the problems and delay treatment, meaning that the client finds it much harder to return to normal. Ignoring the signs could mean that the coaching itself exacerbates a relatively minor psychological problem. Taking too strong an action could lead to the client struggling with the stigma of mental illness in the future. Taking injudicious action in a work-based setting could lead to future job problems, even dismissal. Hence the need to be clear in the rationale behind the choice made for the future of coaching.

There are five routes forward after the discovery of some form of mental health issue (see Table 4.1). Option 3, stop

Table 4.1 **The options**

What next?
1 Continue coaching the client
2 Continue coaching with other support
3 Stop coaching, giving the reasons
4 Stop coaching; support the client whilst they find appropriate other help
5 Take action to initiate appropriate help for the client

coaching, giving the reasons, is the central point of choices and is the safest way forward. It is the most straightforward option, formally ending the relationship with the client who has shown some signs of mental health issues. Moving away from this response, in either direction, needs more detailed consideration.

If the coach is considering option 1 or 2, which means continuing with the coaching relationship, then thought needs to be given to the likely coaching efficacy, practicalities such as the focus of coaching and the personal motivations of the coach for wanting to continue. Rigorous questioning by the coach of their intentions, ideally with the help of a supervisor, will help to ensure that a decision to continue is appropriate and in the best interests of the client. If one of the differentiators between coaching and therapy is that coaching 'Deals with a healthy client desiring a better situation' (Williams 2003: 26), once there is a suspicion that the client no longer fits the term 'healthy' then the onus is on the coach to justify any continuation of the relationship.

With options 4 and 5 the decision has been taken to stop coaching, effectively ending the coaching relationship, and the implications are different. The considerations are about the appropriateness of actions taken beyond the coaching relationship and contract. How will the coach justify taking actions beyond terminating the coaching?

The rationale behind each of the options and specific cases where the choice may be appropriate are considered below.

Continue coaching the client

There will be many cases where continuing to coach the client is appropriate after the recognition of signs of some form of psychological distress. But, if the coach is not comfortable and clear that the plan to continue coaching this client is valid from all viewpoints discussed in Chapter 3, then the coach needs to reflect on the reasoning that this is being considered. Is this a personal issue for the coach such as a difficulty in accepting that coaching cannot benefit everyone all the time or is the coach responding to some neediness in the client for example?

The coach has a duty of care to the client to provide ethical and effective coaching, not to prolong the relationship once it is clear that the client is no longer receiving benefit and not to coach when some other form of help such as counselling or psychotherapy is indicated. There is also the moral question of continuing to charge fees to a client with raised concerns over their emotional state and ability to benefit from the coaching experience.

The first consideration is the wishes of the client. The coach will have talked over their concerns for the emotional or psychological state of the client and the client will have responded in some way. If the client says they wish to continue and their response seems clear and based in reality then consider continuing coaching. However, the fact that the client wants to continue is not, alone, a sufficient reason to carry on. If the client is ambivalent, or unclear, about continuing then it is probably best to stop or take a break, agreeing to revisit the question in the future. It would be best to allow the client to make any future contact; the coach leaves the route to continuing in the future open but does not take steps that may pressure the client to resume coaching.

A second consideration is a judgement on whether the psychological problem is best termed an issue in the coaching or a barrier to coaching. If there is a barrier to coaching then do not continue until the barrier has been removed or it is clear that it can be sidestepped or avoided. If the problem can be termed an issue (such as a trap or turbulence, discussed in Chapter 1), or a barrier that can be avoided, then try to answer the questions in Table 4.2 to add clarity to the decision to continue.

Can the client maintain a separation in their lives between the suffering and the focus of the coaching? The suffering could be either functional or dysfunctional suffering, as described in Chapter 1. There are those who go through the whole of their lives in a perfectly satisfactory manner whilst either avoiding or occasionally becoming distressed by certain psychological aspects of their lives.

Table 4.2 **Questions**

- Is the issue separate from the coaching focus or context?
  - ➤ If the client's problems seem separate from the coaching focus, consider continuing.
  - ➤ If the problems are pervasive or part of the focus of coaching, stop.

- Is the issue temporary, likely to resolve itself in a few weeks?
  - ➤ If the problems are likely to resolve themselves, consider continuing.
  - ➤ If long term or recurring, stop.

- Will the issue be appropriately dealt with elsewhere?
  - ➤ Is the client well-supported elsewhere?
    Consider continuing.
  - ➤ Coaching is not focused on emotional support. If the client has little support, stop.

- How emotionally resilient is the client, are they robust emotionally?
  - ➤ A strong person will cope better with psychological pain, consider continuing.
  - ➤ An emotionally fragile person may struggle, stop.

- How self-aware is the client of this issue?
  - ➤ If the client is aware of the issue, consider continuing.
  - ➤ If the client denies the issue or seems unaware of it stop.

- Does the client have a realistic plan to deal with or cope with this issue?
  - ➤ If a plan is positive, consider continuing.
  - ➤ If no plan to address the issue, stop.

- Is the issue something that may impact on the coach?
  - ➤ If so, stop.

Functional suffering is one likely scenario when continuing to coach could be appropriate: something has happened in the client's life that has caused a psychological upset or disturbance, bereavement for example. With functional suffering, suffering that, however difficult and painful, seems to have a clear and appropriate link to an event, there is a strong likelihood of it going away with time. Business coaching could be beneficial for someone with problems in their personal life, separation or divorce for example. The coach may be able to help the client to maintain and enhance work-based achievements with little impact from personal problems, even though the client could be experiencing quite severe mood swings (anxiety and depression) or be very angry some of the time.

The client's personal support network may impact a decision to continue. Someone with strong supportive relationships is more likely to be able to engage in coaching whilst struggling with psychological issues. This holds true whether the issues are likely to be temporary or more longlasting. A good support network reduces the temptation to use the coaching time for support in those areas that are causing problems.

Does it seem likely that the client is robust enough emotionally to be coached whilst going through the process of functional suffering? This is a judgement call, based on what the coach knows of the client and has a high element of guesswork involved in it. For example, a coach is working with a highly successful businessperson who suffers the unexpected loss of a parent. The client has always appeared an emotionally solid person and they decide to continue as coaching is focused on business-related matters, the idea being that grieving will continue with the support of friends and family and can be separated from work life. The coach needs to be on the lookout for any signs that the client is not able to maintain a focus on the coaching both during and between the sessions because it is impossible to predict, in advance, the course of the grieving process.

Self-awareness is important in any coaching relationship. Once signs of mental illness have emerged the client who shows an understanding of what is going on for them and can, in a way, stand aside and objectively look at their problems is more likely to gain benefit from continuing coaching. Someone with a form of autism, who is able to become aware of the problems they have been having, with relationships for example, may well find coaching extremely beneficial. If they are not really aware that they have any issues, or deny the problem, then the likelihood of coaching helping the client is minimal. Even if the focus of the coaching is separate from the area of the problem, a lack of awareness on the part of the client is a real negative and the coach may wish to reconsider any thoughts of continuing. If it has become clear that a client is abusing drugs or alcohol but seems unaware that this is affecting their emotions all the time, not just when drunk, hungover or high, then coaching could be dangerous rather than helpful. The client could easily use the escape route of their drug of choice rather than work at the changes that the coaching is supposed to bring.

A client who is able to show a sensible level of self-awareness that they have some issues may well be able to think of a plan of how to deal with them in the future. A workable plan reduces concerns over mental health problems and a client who knows how they are going to deal with the issues that have arisen may well be able to continue with the coaching.

A point that must be considered by the professional coach is their own conscious and unconscious reaction to the issues that the client has raised. Is there any chance that the coach's 'own stuff' could get in the way of coaching the client? This is a general rule for coaching in all situations. With the client who has some form of mental health problem a more than normally cautious approach is indicated. Considering offering coaching, or continuing to coach, a client when they have emotional problems does not increase the danger of the coach being influenced by their 'own stuff', but it does increase the likelihood that confusion by the coach on the 'my stuff/your stuff' boundary will have damaging effects. It adds an extra dimension to the complexities of the coaching that may prove to be an effective barrier to reaching goals.

Knowledge of an issue, however functionally separate

from the focus of coaching, can bring problems. Even a seemingly minor matter, in the context of the coaching, may have repercussions. Will the coach overly compensate for the problem, losing the impetus and drive that coaching can bring? Can the client engage with the coach knowing that an issue, possibly perceived as a weakness or embarrassment, has been seen? Will the issue be used as an excuse for not reaching goals and not completing tasks?

In Chapter 5 (Andrea's story), the first scenario concerns a normal grief reaction after a miscarriage. Andrea has not shared her loss with anyone at work. Continuing to coach with this knowledge may lead to difficulties. The coach may be overly considerate and forgiving should Andrea struggle to use the coaching to enhance her work or Andrea may use the sessions for an emotional dump as the coach is someone who knows her secret. An overly sympathetic coach could allow the pain that Andrea is suffering to become a barrier to any effective coaching. It is also possible that Andrea may use her grief to hide behind, as a way to avoid looking at her work patterns. The coach does not know Andrea's normal emotional make-up and will not be able to judge if this is happening, for all the coach knows she may routinely use excuses and blame others for any shortcomings at work, and now she has the 'excuse' of the loss of an unborn child. Anything could be hidden behind the grief, leading to ineffective coaching.

Once signs of a mental health issue have become evident in a client and continuing to coach is the chosen option, be prepared to revisit this choice frequently and be alert for any changes in the client that suggest a different option. The coach needs to be able to justify what they are doing at all times.

Continue coaching with other support

In this context 'other support' is considered to be other professional support and not the normal support offered by friends, family and work colleagues. The major justifications for continuing to coach are similar to option 1 (above); the thought processes on likely efficacy and the practicalities of continuing are similar, with some extra facts that may impact on any future coaching and need consideration.

Option 4, stop coaching; support the client whilst they find other help, discusses the cautious approach needed if continuing to see someone who has problems to ensure that support is offered, not coaching or counselling. It is extremely important with option 2 that the coach is clear what they are offering to the client who is seeing another professional. The question is, 'Am I coaching this client?', not offering support or counselling. If the client can join in the coaching activity without being overly affected by their mental health problems then coaching whilst they get help from someone else can be appropriate.

A clear separation between the focus of the coaching and the psychological problem is needed to justify coaching someone who is under the care of a mental health professional. This separation can be physical and/or psychological. A physical separation could be coaching around work-related issues whilst another professional helps with issues of depression, for example, that are focused in their personal life. A psychological separation could be a client with an obsessive-compulsive disorder who receives help for this from a cognitive behavioural therapist whilst the coaching is focused on other areas where the obsessive behaviour has little impact.

The onus is on the coach to be clear in the justification of continuing, that the coaching is likely to be effective and that the client's return to mental health will not be affected in any way. To consider offering coaching to someone who is receiving help from a mental health professional, whether this is the client's personal physician, a psychiatrist, psychologist, counsellor, therapist, a mental health nurse or other it is vital that the coach has a clear view of the boundaries of what can be offered. A clear and realistic understanding of the likely efficacy of any coaching and a well-thought-through rationale to justify the continuing relationship with the client is needed.

The decision to continue coaching alongside some other form of treatment is a harder choice for the coach and the client than continuing in those cases where the client needs no other support than that offered by friends and family. The more straightforward cases where coaching is likely to be a sensible option will lie in business-related coaching, where the coaching is focused on work-related performance and achievements. This will provide one clear differentiator and boundary for the coaching and could be advantageous to the client and a sponsoring organisation in helping the client to maintain their work and work-based achievements whilst getting help for a psychological problem. By the very nature of the holistic approach taken by most life and personal coaches it will be harder to justify continuing and much harder to avoid crossing the coaching–therapy boundary. Speciality 'niche market' coaches will need to follow the process laid out here before deciding on the justification of coaching a client whilst another professional is seeing them for their mental health problems.

Although the coach may have been instrumental in the client seeking help, the coaching must now take second place to treatment. Concerns have been raised over the mental health of the client and taking care of this takes precedence over coaching goals.

Primacy in the professional relationships with the client must lie with the mental health professional. Any client who has been seen by a mental health professional will have undergone a far more rigorous mental state examination or assessment than the coach can provide and they will have a fuller picture of the circumstances and history of the symptoms. They may be aware of a history of mental health problems, of trigger factors and the potential risk. Medication may have been prescribed and a treatment regime put in place to help the client. The coach is unlikely to have any specific knowledge of this, other than comments from the client, and will need to accept that appropriate and professional treatment is being given.

It would be sensible to check that the client has told the mental health professional that they are also talking to a coach. They may need to know this information, they may suggest that the coaching stops or leave any decision to the client. For the coach, the knowledge that the client has talked about the coaching does reduce any chance that the client may be tempted to keep these two, possibly conflicting, relationships separate. This openness about what is happening reduces the danger that the client may manipulate the two relationships to avoid accepting and dealing with mental health problems. The coach must be cautious that they do not collude with the client, however inadvertently, in their attempts to avoid treatment.

Coaching alongside another professional can be quite appropriate if care is taken to avoid confusion for the client and working in opposition to treatment. The following points offer a summary, but, if the coach has any concerns or reservations, then it is best if the coaching stops:

- Be clear on what is being offered.
  - ➢ Be clear that coaching is being offered.
- Focus on offering effective coaching.
  - ➢ Be ready to stop if this is not working.
- Avoid exploring the psychological issue during coaching.
  - ➢ Asking about the problem could lead to confusion.
- Coaching could have a negative impact on mental health treatment.
  - ➢ If there is any hint that the coaching is working against other support, then stop.
- Be aware that some clients find 'talking therapies' painful and hard work.
  - ➢ If the client starts to talk about their therapy in a negative way then be aware that they may be looking for an excuse to stop, take care not to collude in this.

Stop coaching, giving the reasons

Once signs of some form of mental health issue have surfaced in the coaching client the decision to stop coaching is probably the cleanest way forwards. This choice allows the coach to end the relationship formally by stating the reasoning behind the decision and offering the view that coaching will not be of benefit. If appropriate there could be a general suggestion of seeking help elsewhere.

This choice can always be seen as the 'best practice position', a safe and sensible course of action whenever signs of psychological problems have been seen. Stopping coaching, though, may be an unnecessarily cautious route in some cases. But, it is a good starting point in the decision-making process. As detailed above, there are many considerations to take into account to move from a decision to stop to a decision to continue and detailed below are the considerations needed to decide if anything more than just ending coaching is appropriate. Stopping coaching may, alone, not be sufficient in these cases and some further action on the part of the coach is needed.

In some cases, particularly those involving a third party contract, some thought may be needed around the mechanics of ending coaching – what reason will be given for ending? The coach and client need to be in agreement as to the story that will be given in order to avoid confusion. Problems could follow if the coach said that the client had mental health issues, whilst the client had decided to keep these private and had told line management that he, or she, did not think coaching was going to work, or did not get on with the coach. The reason given to others for the ending of coaching needs to respect the client's confidentiality and if the client wishes to maintain confidentiality around the real reason a simple statement that neither party felt that coaching was going to be beneficial at this time should suffice.

Should the client decide to seek further coaching in the future a sensibly cautious approach is best. If the barrier to coaching has been removed and the issue resolved then coaching could continue as long as both parties are sure that the previous experience and knowledge of that issue will not impact on the coaching. If there is a suspicion that any of the potential pitfalls discussed in options 1 and 2 may get in the way of effective coaching then contacting another coach can be suggested.

Stop coaching; support the client whilst they find appropriate other help

The responsibility for the client's future lies with the client. It is the client's choice whether or not to ask for help with a psychological or mental health issue. However potentially damaging to self or others the problem may be, there are few instances where the medical profession can force the client to accept treatment. Medical practitioners are often faced with a difficult period of waiting and patience as a clearly unwell patient avoids treatment or denies the need for treatment.

Whilst it may appear the kindest thing to do, offering continuing support after the coaching has stopped has implications and needs thought before being offered. One way of looking at this is to think about the relationship with the client. If no coaching is taking place, what justification is there for any continuing relationship? What is the relationship that is being offered and why? Some coaches may be in a position to offer the client assistance in finding appropriate help, with local knowledge of support services for example. But, without the information found with a full psychological assessment it may be difficult to judge whether any suggestions of help being made are the best choice for this client and so a cautious approach may be needed. The safest approach is to suggest a visit to their own doctor who will be better placed to judge what, if any, mental health support is needed.

If the best choice seems to be to support the client on their route to appropriate help for their psychological problems and the choice holds true after taking into account all the viewpoints and considerations explored in Chapter 3, then this support is best offered with a light touch. Attempts by the coach to push the need for support or judge the type of support needed could be damaging for the client. The client may resist the need to seek alternative support or look for inappropriate support for their problems.

It is probably best if the coach only takes on this type of role if no one else is available. Supporting a client whilst they seek other forms of help for their problems blurs the professional boundaries of what the coach offers to clients in general and to the supported client in particular. There is probably little distinction between coaching and any of the other forms of 'helping by talking' approaches such as counselling in the general population and by maintaining a relationship after the discovery of a possible barrier to coaching there is the risk that the client may consider that they are receiving help for their problems. If the client gained the impression that they were receiving treatment rather than being helped to find an appropriate way forward the coach could be accused of offering therapy outside of their competence, training and, perhaps, legal entitlement. The mental health licensing section of the State of Colorado (USA) has an article titled 'Coaching: Is this Considered the Practice of Psychotherapy?' (Martinez, 2004), which explores the boundary between coaching and counselling or psychotherapy from a legal perspective and the coach could, inadvertently, cross the boundary when choosing this way forward. Focusing on the following points will help:

- Be clear on what is being offered.
  - ➤ Be clear that coaching has stopped.
- Focus on offering information, not advice.
  - ➤ Sources of local help may be useful to the client, advice suggests a diagnosis, which is inappropriate.
- Avoid exploring the issue further.
  - ➤ Talking about problems could lead to confusion that treatment is being given.
- Maintain contact for a minimal length of time.
  - ➤ The goal is for the client to receive appropriate care, promptly.
- Do not accept payment.
  - ➤ Payment suggests a professional relationship, which no longer exists as coaching is not taking place.

Take action to initiate appropriate help for the client

With option 5 (Table 4.1), where the coach decides that the best course is to take action on behalf of the client, the coach needs to ensure that this decision has been taken thoughtfully, as there may be consequences. By taking action the coach has moved from a position of valuing the client's autonomy and their ability to make effective choices to taking control of the client's life. The goal in taking action on the client's behalf is to pass on responsibility to a more appropriate person. A secondary goal would be to provide a safety net for the coach in being seen to have taken appropriate professional action by informing others of concerns for a disturbed client. By taking action on behalf of the client the coach has stepped beyond the boundaries of the coaching relationship and has judged that something has happened that means that the client can no longer take responsibility for their life.

With a formal contract for coaching, agreed in advance by all parties, there should be clear boundaries on confidentiality and the cases where the coach may break this without the client's permission and, as discussed in Chapter 3, statements of ethics and standards are helpful in stating the 'rules' for breaking confidentiality and when to take action.

The action that is taken may range from passing on responsibility to another in a work-based setting, perhaps human resources, management or a staff welfare officer. It could be a relative or other who is in a position to influence the individual to access appropriate help, the client's personal doctor for example. If necessary it will be the emergency services: a police, ambulance or medical emergency response. A consideration will be whether the newly involved person or system will take what has happened seriously. For example, a client has shown signs of suicidal intent in the session but when asked by another says: 'I'm fine, thanks, everything is OK, no of course I'm not going to do anything silly.' A mental health professional is likely to explore what has happened and come to their own conclusions, a relative or work colleague may accept the client's view on face value, perhaps thinking that the coach is being rather dramatic. The coach may need to be firm and clear in articulating their concerns, following the guidelines in Chapter 3. A psychotic episode such as Carl's (Chapter 7) could be quite brief and he could have appeared normal to another person a short time later; the coach would need to be happy that the next person in the chain to the client getting appropriate help will follow through and not just ignore the issues.

After taking this decision, following the guidelines in Chapter 3, coaching and the coaching contract is effectively over. The responsibility of the coach lies in passing on any duty to another person or system. Once this has been

achieved the coach removes themselves from the relationship and any desire for further contact needs to be viewed
with suspicion by the coach themselves. After introducing
the client to another agency the coach does not make contact, does not call to see how things are going, or interfere
in the client's life in any way. The act of taking action on
the client's behalf, perhaps breaking confidentiality to
inform another of the client's behaviour, has ended the
coaching contract. Without the activity of coaching any
thoughts of and attempts to justify contact must be viewed
with suspicion, as meeting the needs of the coach rather
than client, after all there no longer exists a coaching client,
just a relative stranger who has problems.

But, the coach may be emotionally affected by contact
with someone who has problems of the severity that action
needs to be taken. The place for these emotions is in supervision. Talking over the actions and feelings with a consultant
helps to normalise feelings around the action taken. The
coach may question themselves on whether they made
the correct decision – did they overreact – or be normally
concerned as to the outcome and want to know if the client
is OK, or, at least, getting the proper treatment. These
thoughts should be talked over with someone appropriate,
not acted on by contacting the client or the client's family.

If the client contacts the coach at a later date then any
response should be extremely cautious. The client may telephone with thanks for the action taken, the coach accepts
the thanks but does not get involved. A client may contact
the coach to resume coaching, the coach needs to be cautious, there will be little knowledge as to the progress the
client has made or what other professionals are involved in
the client's care. The coach will not know how honest the
client is being in their judgement of their mental state.
The technically correct answer to a client requesting a
resumption of coaching is to suggest contacting another
coach. Too many extraneous issues may be present in any
future relationship for coaching to continue in a normal
and appropriate fashion. The coach is likely to be highly
aware of and on the lookout for signs of a repetition of the
problem. The client may see the coach as their saviour, an

unhelpful and unrealistic viewpoint that could be a substantial barrier to the coaching. The coach needs to just say how pleased they are to hear how well the client is doing and suggest it would be best to speak to another coach, if necessary say something about it being against their code of conduct. If absolutely pushed by the client, the coach should be firm and say no.

A final type of contact that the coach needs to be aware of is the client who starts to take steps to 'punish' the coach. The term 'punish' is used rather than 'complaint' because contact may not be through the channels of a governing body or via the legal process. A formal complaint may well be easier to deal with than an informal attempt to punish the coach for their actions. The coach will have a forum to state their case for the actions taken and professionally competent persons will judge these. The informal method could be attempts to question the coach's professionalism, spreading rumours that they aren't any good, or it could be through some form of harassment. Whilst these may be unlikely extremes of behaviour, the coach needs to be aware of the potential. Discussing the event with a supervisor and keeping clear and detailed notes are important safeguards for the coach as well as the professionally competent course of action.

Learning points

- Keep notes.
- Discuss 'what next' with a supervisor or colleague.
- If coaching ends due to a psychological issue, be cautious with any further contact.
- Be professional, not personal, this is a client, not a friend.
- Be clear that coaching is being offered if continuing to see a client with possible mental health problems.
- Be certain that coaching is being undertaken, not counselling or psychotherapy.
- 'What next' is the most important part of the process of working with someone with mental health issues.

SECTION 2

What's being said?

This section is structured around fictitious 'clients'. Each chapter follows a similar format. The client is introduced with background and context for the coaching. This leads into dialogue between the coach and client. Examples of questioning are used to help open up what may be happening as two or more possible scenarios develop.

Interspersed in the dialogue are comments about what might be going on and reasons for taking the questioning approach. The clues as to what might be happening are highlighted as well as the rationale for thinking this.

As each scenario unfolds the ethics and choices are discussed with suggestions of appropriate ways forward.

Developing each client scenario in more than one way emphasises how people can show similar signs that have different possible diagnoses and ways forward. This helps to show how exploration can assist in gathering information to gain a more complete picture before deciding what to do.

The written dialogue may appear false and stilted in places; an attempt has been made not to use slang, colloquialisms and regional language variations. A key point to be aware of when listening to someone is a change in use of language, for example someone experiencing anxiety may start to talk more freely, using more robust language and slang for instance. For others, slang, bad language and loose phraseology will be the norm and a change to more precise language control may be an indicator that something is going on that warrants further exploration. Of necessity the dialogue is relatively brief; in real life the suggestions that something is wrong may be interspersed with periods of normal conversation.

5

Andrea's story

This chapter explores the story of Andrea, showing how an appropriate, though painful, grief reaction and a serious episode of depression could develop.

An external coach is asked to talk to Andrea, a smart, intelligent and articulate middle-ranking executive in a multi-national organisation. The coach has worked with several other employees in the organisation and has an understanding of the organisation's culture.

The coach has heard about Andrea in conversation as a successful manager and role model with an expectation of a future including promotion and more responsibility. The brief was to help her to manage her team after an unexpected decline in performance.

The initial meeting between the coach and Andrea was quite difficult as she seemed resistant to both the need for help and there being a problem with her team's performance and was generally uninterested in coaching. Although her verbal communication was almost perfect, when looked at as a whole the coach saw a sad person whose facial expression and body language did not match the words she was using. Andrea was not the dynamic manager the coach had been expecting.

Andrea talked about her team being cohesive, successful and loyal, but in the past tense. She said little about the team in the present.

After the first meeting the coach thought that the unexpectedly poor performance of Andrea's team had come

as a shock to her and that a good starting point would be to
explore what had changed.

Andrea was still quite low at the next session and the
following dialogue developed:

Coach: 'As I understand it, things were going well until
           quite recently, what's changed?'
Andrea: 'Well, it was great last year, we were doing really
           well, everyone was working hard and we were top
           of the tree.'
Coach: 'So, what's changed?'
Andrea: 'I don't get any support now.'
Coach: 'Support from whom?'
Andrea: 'Anyone . . .'
           ['Anyone', an unusual response from Andrea
           and the first sign to the coach that there may
           be something unusual going on. As the
           coach's warning bells start to ring, her
           response is checked.]
Coach: 'Anyone?'
Andrea: 'You know, the boyfriend, the boss, my Mum, even
           the troops . . .'
           [Andrea's response tells the coach that her
           low mood is quite pervasive through most
           aspects of her life.]
Coach: 'So it's not just at work then?'
           [This questioning has shown that Andrea's
           low mood is of fairly recent onset ('great last
           year') and not just a work issue, two of the
           three P's of questioning.]
Andrea: [No comment, just a shrug of the shoulders]
Coach: 'What can you do about it?'
           [Does Andrea have any plans?]
Andrea: 'There's nothing to do . . .'

At this point the coach has several pieces of information
'stored in the corner':

1 The incongruence of the expectation of a dynamic
manager with her low mood and lack of interest in
coaching.
2 Her low mood and sadness in both the first two sessions.

3 Something has changed ('. . . it was great last year . . .').
4 It's not just at work.
5 Andrea cannot see a way out of it.

It is quite likely that the coach would revisit some of these areas to check out Andrea's responses and to gather more information, perhaps asking about the support that Andrea had historically. Questioning further gives Andrea the opportunity to either confirm the coach's developing suspicions that something is wrong or to refute them and start to engage in the coaching. It is important to recognise that getting to this point in conversation will usually take more than one meeting, for the relationship to develop and trust to be established.

Because the issues are so all-embracing the indications are that something quite fundamental has changed for Andrea and this is more than a work-related issue.

If the lack of support was due to changes in either management or focus at work, coaching may well be helpful, even though Andrea is showing a low mood at the moment. She could be helped to look at her side of any changes and plan a way forward.

Continuing the dialogue:

> [Rather than following on from 'There's nothing to do', which is a very depressing statement, the coach goes back a step with the following question.]

Coach: 'What support did you used to get?'

> [This question aims to link to a time, for Andrea, when things were different. The coach is testing out their warning bells.]

Andrea: 'Oh, I don't know . . .' [coupled with a shaky voice and a tearful expression]

Coach: 'Andrea, I'm wondering if something else has been happening recently?'

By now there have been many pointers that something is amiss and the coach has checked some of these out by careful and sympathetic questioning. A straightforward request for information, delivered in a non-threatening way, is probably the best way for the coach to find out what is really happening for the client.

In this case Andrea went on to tell the coach that she suffered an early miscarriage some months ago and that she has not shared this with anyone at work. Her loss and grief are the main focus of life and they have affected her work.

The issues to consider for the coach and coaching are:

1 Should coaching continue, is it safe for both the coach and the client and is it likely to be of benefit?
2 How can Andrea best be helped at the moment?
3 What is the way forward?

These issues are described further below:

1 In this scenario it is easy to see that the grief is of recent origin (some months ago) and Andrea has not been able to resolve it yet. So, it sounds quite a normal and reasonable grief reaction. This type of issue will usually respond to either some supportive help or short-term counselling (for example).

It is unlikely that coaching will be of any benefit until her mood has lifted sufficiently for her to be able to focus on work in an objective and more enthusiastic manner.

Coaching itself will probably be best put on hold for a period until Andrea is in a position to take advantage of it. The coach will then be well positioned to help her re-establish her professional position if that is what she chooses. With grieving such as this, it is possible that telling the coach what happened and finding someone appropriate to support her may very quickly allow Andrea to become able to function normally most of the time and return to being the manager she was.

2 Encourage her to seek help. This could be as resource information, a visit to her doctor or to talk to a suitably qualified counsellor.

Although many coaches will have both the training and ability to manage this type of grief, it is probably best to avoid trying to do more than offer suggested resources and ways forward. Trying to move to a therapeutic relationship will change the boundaries and future working relationship. The client organisation has asked for coaching for an employee, not counselling. Andrea is most likely to make best use of any talking therapy she engages in at a neutral venue rather than her workplace during a working day.

3 This leaves the formality of managing a break in coaching with the sponsoring organisation. An issue for the coach is confidentiality. Andrea has, so far, chosen not to share her grief with anyone at work and the coach needs to respect this. This needs to be clearly and honestly talked through. It is important that Andrea and her coach come to agreement on how to handle cessation, or a break, in coaching.

A different direction

This scenario could well have developed in a different direction; with the same introduction and first meeting something far more worrying and potentially serious could have developed. For the second session Andrea arrived 15 minutes late.

Coach:	'As I understand it, things were going well until quite recently, what's changed?'
Andrea:	'Oh, they're doing fine really.'
Coach:	'But not as well as expected?'
Andrea:	[No comment, no eye contact, sad expression and body language]
Coach:	'What has been happening?'
Andrea:	'Oh, I don't know.'
	[As in the first session, Andrea appears generally sad, she also seems to be differentiating between herself and her team ('Oh they're doing fine really.'). She has not answered two direct questions.]
Coach:	'How do you feel about the future?'
	[The coach attempts to find out where this sadness sits with Andrea, does she see it as a temporary state? Looking to the future and asking about plans is a common task in

> coaching and this is an example of the coach testing out what is being heard, allowing Andrea an opportunity to talk rationally about her work.]

Andrea: 'Well, you know, I don't know, it's not clear . . .'

Coach: 'Where do you see yourself in a couple of years' time?'

> [This is developing into a difficult conversation, again the coach attempts to allow Andrea to give a clear answer to a direct question.]

Andrea: 'Not here.'

> [The use of open questions can achieve a lot – it can also open a can of worms. What does Andrea mean by 'not here', it may mean not with this company or it may be an expression of a suicidal idea. These are, perhaps, the two extremes. It would not be unusual to find yourself in a situation where Andrea now breaks down and pours out her heart to you.]

Coach: 'Where else then?'

Andrea: 'I don't know.'

Coach: 'What's your plan?'

Andrea: 'I can't do this job, I'm not good enough, I can't think straight, I don't know where I'm going.'

> [By now it is becoming very clear that something is going on and that this is more than a client who does not want coaching, does not see the need for coaching or does not feel comfortable talking to the coach.]

Coach: 'What's happened?'

Andrea: 'I'm just so tired.'

Coach: 'I thought the team was doing quite well?'

Andrea: 'They don't need me any more . . .'

At this point the coach should have alarm bells ringing very loudly and clearly. Andrea has done a number of things that the coach has picked up as warning signs as listed below. These have been checked out and several opportunities given for Andrea to respond in a clear and rational manner.

1 She was late for the session (punctuality is the expected culture of the organisation).
2 She is talking in a very depressed way and not answering direct questions.
3 Her general appearance and body language add to this.
4 She was unable to look to the future.
5 She was evasive and non-communicative with many of her responses.

These types of responses are typical of someone with a significant depressive illness. There may be suicidal thoughts or intentions, and this woman needs professional help urgently.

In this scenario, the coach probably needs to take action. First, Andrea needs to be told of the coach's concerns in straightforward language: 'What you are saying is really giving me concerns. Have you seen your doctor recently?' This is a clear statement of the coach's concerns and a direct question, and, again, allows Andrea the choice to respond. There could be a scenario where such a question would 'shock' the client into realising what they had been saying and change the pattern of conversation.

The client should be strongly advised to seek urgent medical help and in a situation such as this it is probably appropriate to tell someone else in the organisation what has happened. Tell the client this is what you are going to do and why. Be clear in communicating this.

High achievers with a depressive illness will often maintain a superficial facade of coping; they may still be smart and punctual. Signs from them will be in their attitude and output at work. As coaches we are asked to work with people whose effectiveness at work may have declined and one reason for this can be a depressive illness.

When a coach experiences a client such as this and takes action there are a number of steps for them to take:

1 Making clear and accurate notes of the sessions. Making sure that facts are recorded that back up suspicions.
2 Discussing the case with their supervisor, mentor or other experienced professional.
3 Making contact with the person in the organisation

responsible for hiring them and talking over what you have done and why.

Conclusions

This chapter has looked at two scenarios that had similar beginnings but very different outcomes. The implications for coaching are very different.

With the first case of uncomplicated grief, the actions of the coach are less critical. If the coach takes no action, Andrea's situation is unlikely to be made worse and, should the decision be to continue with the coaching, then it may help her to return to normality for the work part of her life.

In the second scenario of a severe depressive episode, continuing coaching could have potentially serious consequences, intensifying for Andrea just how different life is now to how it used to be. Highlighting the possibilities that Andrea can achieve at work through coaching could have dangerous outcomes by making her present depressive state seem far worse than it is and emphasising the hopelessness of her present life.

Learning points

- Explore unusual responses.
- Is it a work-related or whole-life issue?
- How long has the problem been around?
- Give the client an opportunity to respond 'in reality'.
- Address the issues clearly, honestly and openly.
- Coaching is unlikely to be helpful when your client has a low mood.
- It may sometimes be necessary to take action outside the boundaries of the coaching contract.

6

Brian's life unravels

Brian has issues of grieving that may be more complex than usual and a hidden problem with drink makes coaching erratic.

Brian is a successful 53-year-old businessman head-hunted for his current role last year. His task is to complete an important project in a relatively short period of time. This was a task he had done in the past and one he was ideally suited for. However, things were going badly and he hadn't achieved what was expected. The company coach was brought in to facilitate change within the team.

The coach met with the whole team and then with each member individually. Brian appears dynamic, a good talker and everything his CV promised. The first task that is agreed is that Brian needs to produce a detailed list of priorities and objectives to help the team focus on the project.

Superficially, Brian appears competent, however the rest of the team paint a very different picture. Within two months of the project beginning they had noticed a significant change in his behaviour. He started arriving late for work and leaving early. A woman member of the team observes that he is wearing the same shirt for several days at a time, and his PA despairs of ever getting him to the right meeting at the right time.

The coach decides to focus on some individual work with Brian and meets him for the first one-to-one session.

Coach: 'How did the priorities and objectives go?'
Brian: 'It didn't.'

Coach: 'Didn't?'
Brian: 'They should never have asked me to do this; I'll
          never be up to the job. I should just resign and go
          quietly. I don't think I've ever been as good as
          people think. I've just conned my way to the top.'
          [The session has immediately taken an
          unusual direction. The first priority is to try
          to find out if this is a temporary problem
          with a solution or has long-term conse-
          quences for Brian and the project.]
Coach: 'How long have you been thinking like this?'
Brian: 'It's always been like this.'
Coach: 'Brian, that can't be true, I've seen your CV and
          we've talked about your previous successes.'
Brian: 'I told you, it was all a confidence trick.'
Coach: 'Are you telling me your CV is untrue?'
          [The coach is asking about the rationality of
          Brian's response. Check out for any factual
          reason for the client saying unusual things
          before exploring for deeper meaning.]
Brian: 'No, no, it all happened, it just seems so meaning-
          less now.'
          [Something has changed for Brian; it is more
          important to find out when this change hap-
          pened than to explore the depth or scope of
          Brian's response. Although 'What's mean-
          ingless?' is an appropriate person-centred
          question, the coach needs to know how long
          Brian has felt like this and asks:]
Coach: 'When did it become meaningless?'
Brian: 'January.'
Coach: 'That's very precise, so, things started to change
          just after you started here. What happened?'
Brian: 'My father died at Christmas and it's taking me
          ages to sort everything out.'
          [A clear indicator has emerged of a quite
          recent major life event.]
Coach: 'I'm really sorry to hear that, it must be difficult,
          were you very close?'
Brian: 'We lived together, it was just father and I.'

Brian tells the coach of being an only child, his mother dying when he was a teenager and that he has always lived with his father and never married or had a serious relationship.

From a coaching perspective there are indications that Brian may not be able to function adequately enough to engage in the coaching. But, this was just one session; in the previous meeting Brian had appeared far more positive. Having heard and responded to the warning bells the coach waits until the next session to find out how changeable Brian's mood is.

Nothing specific needs to be done at the moment about Brian's grieving, but the coach has a job to do and e-mails a reminder about the priorities and objectives list.

Next session:

Coach: 'Did you get chance to work on your priorities and objectives?'

Brian: 'This is what I've done.'

[He passes over a few handwritten notes.]

Coach: 'What do you want to achieve from these?'

Brian: 'Oh, I don't know.'

[Brian has shown his low mood and lack of interest again. The thought that the previous session could have been an isolated incident has been proved false. Coaching is not going to achieve anything with Brian as he is.]

Coach: 'You seem very low again, Brian.'

Brian: 'I can't do anything at the moment. Life's so empty now dad's gone, there doesn't seem any point.'

[A very depressing statement that needs checking out.]

Coach: 'Point in what?

Brian: 'Work, this project just seems so meaningless.'

[Reassuring for the coach, the client feels that there doesn't seem any point in work, rather than in life as a whole. It seems clear that there is no benefit in the coaching as it stands and the coach starts to explore the wider context of Brian's life to help decide what to do.]

Coach: 'What can you do about it?'
                  [Is there any sign of a plan?]
Brian: 'I suppose I hoped that things would just happen, without me having to do anything.'
Coach: 'Work seems really hard at the moment, what's it like at home?'
                  [Widening the perspective of the questioning, the coach is trying to get some ideas for the way to proceed.]
Brian: 'The same really, it's so empty without dad, there's no one there. At first I was busy sorting things out and my aunt came to stay but she's gone home and I don't seem to be able to get on with anything, it's as though my life's stopped too.'

The coach has a clear-enough picture of Brian's grieving to know that coaching is not going to offer a solution to either Brian's problems or the company's needs to manage the project. Brian needs to get some support for his feelings, but he seems to be isolated in his personal life, so, professional help may be indicated. From a medical perspective the recent onset of the symptoms may lead to a suggestion of some time off work just to allow the normal process of grieving to run its course. An abnormal grief reaction is often thought of as one that continues for many months or years. But, Brian has told the coach of the unusually close relationship with his father and this may suggest that Brian is already experiencing an abnormal grief reaction and he does not have access to a support system of friends and family.

The key to the way forward is Brian's attitude, interest in and ability to ask for help. With someone feeling so helpless there may be a lack of motivation to search for help and Brian may just drift into apathy as the easiest thing to do. For the coach it would be sensible to start by asking if Brian has seen his doctor, or another professional.

Two key points are:

- Does Brian recognise that the death of his father is affecting him so profoundly?
- Is he able to see the benefits of asking for help?

If Brian shows little interest in seeking help then the best option is probably to strongly suggest a visit to his doctor.

Within this scenario the needs of the organisation should be considered. Management is aware that Brian is not achieving and the coach is also working with the team. It may be that the place for coaching is to focus on the rest of the team whilst Brian receives help elsewhere or resolves his issues. The company may have an Employee Assistance Programme (EAP) or similar arrangement to support those with problems where Brian could be referred. Should the decision be for Brian to continue at work whilst getting support then there may be a place for coaching support to help him focus on his tasks and manage the team, but the coach will need to be on the lookout for signs of deterioration in Brian's ability to work.

A fake or something more?

With a similar background to the first scenario, the coaching develops in a different way in this second scenario.

Coach: 'How did the priorities and objectives go?'
Brian: 'It didn't.'
Coach: 'Didn't?'
Brian: 'They should never have asked me to do this; I'll never be up to the job. I should just resign and go quietly. I don't think I've ever been as good as people think. I've just conned my way to the top.'

> [The session has immediately taken an unusual direction. The first priority is to try to find out if this is a temporary problem with a solution or has long-term consequences for Brian and the project.]

Coach: 'How long have you been thinking like this?'
Brian: 'It's always been like this.'
Coach: 'Like what?'
Brian: 'I just take on too much and I can't cope.'
Coach: 'How about breaking the job down into manageable chunks?'

[This was the coach's earlier idea about a priorities list, helping Brian to add some structure and focus to his role.]

Brian: 'I know what to do, I just can't do it.'

After this Brian seems to settle into a seemingly more positive attitude and works with the coach on prioritising. After the session the coach is left puzzled and with some concerns about Brian's negative attitude, wondering about the stress he seems to be under and if there is any substance to Brian thinking he is a fake.

Brian misses a session and when the coach telephones to find out why is told that Brian has not come in today, without any reason being given. The coach learns that Brian is becoming unreliable with frequent days off and late arrivals.

At the next session, Brian seems to want to make amends for his earlier attitude, saying he was exhausted, he appears to be actively working with the coach and is very upbeat with plans of what he will do and by when, but, he has not produced a detailed list of priorities and objectives.

At this stage in the coaching it has become clear that Brian has some emotional instability. With his negative views and changeable attitude, he is not producing the expected results and is becoming, or is, unreliable and erratic. The coach has some concerns but there is no focus for these, nothing has come out to suggest that Brian has any specific mental health issues or personal problems other than him saying he was exhausted, so, maybe, he is under a lot of stress at the moment. As Brian has only recently joined the company the coach has no idea whether Brian is usually like this, a difficult personality who people put up with because he achieves results as his CV suggests, or that something has changed for Brian and he has become unstable and erratic.

The picture that the coach is building up from other team members is that Brian is very erratic, moody and unreliable one minute and then great, dynamic and full of energy just shortly afterwards. The coach knows that management and human resources are becoming increasingly concerned about his time keeping and lack of reliability, but it is not the job of the coach at this stage to try to address these. The coach's responsibility lies in working with the team to produce results.

The coach cancels the next session. The next morning the coach goes to Brian's office to apologise and rearrange the session. Brian is there, looking quite dishevelled and tired, but doesn't seem bothered by the cancellation and talks about arranging a meeting for the next week as he is very busy. Brian's PA says that he is available now as his next meeting has just been cancelled and he has nothing on for the rest of the morning. Brian does not appear very happy about this but agrees.

The session starts with Brian being quite lethargic and unresponsive, he does not look well, either tired or perhaps he has a cold. After about ten minutes his mobile telephone rings and Brian answers. He tells the coach he needs to take the call and will come back in a few minutes. The coach is left wondering whether he will.

Brian returns and seems a different person, more upbeat, happier and willing to take part in the session.

Coach: 'That phone call must have been good news, you seem full of energy now.'

> [The coach hopes that in noticing the change Brian might be helped to find triggers for his erratic behaviour.]

Brian: 'It was nothing, anyway I thought your job was to make sure the project is completed, not to question my personal life.'

> [A surprisingly aggressive response to the coach asking a question that Brian has read as an intrusion into his personal life.]

Coach: 'I'm sorry, it's just that you seem so much happier than at the start of the session.'

After the session the coach realises that there is an element of going through the motions in the coaching and a strong sense that Brian has something to hide. Although there hasn't been a return of the low mood seen in the first session or an explanation of what Brian meant about being a fake, the coaching is not going well.

At the next session the coach focuses on clear and simple goal setting, with measurable and achievable steps. Brian seems to work with this and comes up with suggestions and priorities to complete the project. For the coach this feels like coaching someone new to the job, not working with an experienced and senior manager. Putting this together with information from working with other team members the coach comes to the conclusion that no one is managing and leading the team.

Before the coach has to decide how to continue, Brian is suspended for drinking at work.

There have been many clues to this in the sessions, but nothing tangible that a coach could be expected to pick up on. His increasingly erratic behaviour and the discrepancy between how he presents himself some of the time amidst a growing picture of lack of care, mood swings and a sense of hiding give pointers to something being wrong.

The most likely way that it will become clear that a person has an alcohol problem is by being caught out, in this instance by drinking at work. There could be an accident, a drink-driving offence or some other disclosure, which means that there is no longer a way to hide the issue. If the coach had confronted Brian with any suspicions he would probably have responded by denial, possibly aggressively. Even if the coach had smelt alcohol on Brian's breath after he left the room to take a telephone call and commented on this, Brian is unlikely to have changed his behaviour. More likely would be for Brian to deny it and then avoid the coach, in fear of being exposed.

In this scenario there is nothing further for the coach to do except to learn from the experience.

If it becomes clear that a client is drinking inappropriately on a regular basis there may be issues of safety, to self and others, to consider. This is particularly relevant in a work-based setting and management may need to be informed. What, if anything, to do in a private coaching setting is much harder and may hinge on a view of how capable the client is to take care of themselves. With or without the label of alcoholism, anyone drinking heavily on a daily basis, and throughout the day, not just in the evening, will gain no benefit from coaching. As was seen with Brian, any attempts to coach will be erratic and frustrating. A suggestion of seeing a doctor or other specialist is appropriate but without an active desire to change the drinking habits the client is unlikely to take up this offer until forced by circumstances to face the problem.

The way that Brian is behaving in this scenario could have had other causes. There could be an underlying depressive illness, a personality disorder or other mental health problem. There could be a link in the first scenario, of bereavement, where the death of his father was the trigger to excessive drinking. Alternatively, drinking may be a pattern for Brian when under pressure and he has just been lucky not to be caught out so far.

Conclusions

Brian's life unravelled in both these scenarios.

In the first, a sequence of events that no one could have predicted led to his inability to function as expected and as the cause or trigger event became clear, a way forward could be found. It is impossible to predict whether a period of grieving would be followed by Brian returning to normal, or functioning as he did whilst his father was alive. Coaching would have no benefit in the short term, until his mood had lifted and he could focus on work again.

'A fake or something more?' developed into a very confusing picture for the coach. 'It just wasn't right', may be the best way of summing it up. Feeling something isn't right, but without any specifics, may lead to a conclusion of mental health problems or events may unfold which make this clear. Sometimes a coach, or other professional, will work with someone where the difficulties only become clear afterwards. The coach may find out, perhaps by chance, or may never know.

Learning points

- People can change at any age.
- People may not appear as expected.
- Occasionally this will be due to a mental health problem.
- Look for a trigger event.
- Coaching can be very confusing.
- There may be nothing obvious, it's just not right.
- Problems may become clear outside of coaching.

7

Carl and his relationships

Three complex scenarios develop with Carl's story: of Asperger's syndrome (high functioning autism), a psychotic illness and a shy, isolated young man who struggles to relate to others.

A successful and innovative high technology company has a history of attracting the brightest and most promising post-graduate students to its research and development department. The company offers a fast-track development programme to all the new employees at this level. This involves continuing technical training, training in business skills and support and development of Emotional Intelligence for those on the programme.

The coach is employed by the company to provide training in the emotional side of corporate life (team work, relationships, time management, etc.) and one-to-one coaching. It is a rolling programme, which means that new employees join an existing group soon after starting. The coach first meets Carl in a couple of workshops and notes that he is very quiet and does not join in; this is put down to shyness.

The coach has a one-to-one session booked with Carl and reviews what is known about this new employee beforehand. Carl is extraordinarily bright and technically competent. There was competition from several places to offer him a job; management is excited about having attracted him. The coach's technical training colleagues are very impressed with his abilities.

When Carl arrives in the training department the coach

is in the office talking to a colleague. Carl walks straight past and into the coach's private office.

The coach follows to find Carl sitting in a chair in front of the desk, looking straight ahead.

Coach: 'Hello Carl, thanks for coming and I'm sorry I'm a few minutes late, shall we sit over here?' [Indicating the armchairs in the corner.]

        [Carl doesn't answer, but seems to tense, showing he has heard the coach.]

Coach: 'OK' [sitting at the desk opposite Carl.]

        [The coach starts a preamble about spending some time together, just getting to know one another.]

Coach: 'So, what do you think you might like to get from our time together?'

Carl: 'What I need is to find a way for BC 545 to communicate with LM version 3 without an operator.'

Coach: 'Sorry, Carl, I'm not a techie. I can't help you with those sorts of things, but maybe I can help you find a way forwards?'

Carl: 'Oh.' [Looks over his shoulder towards the door.]

Coach: 'Perhaps you'd like to tell me what it's like for you working here?'

        [Carl looks down into his lap, his body language has been very still, almost rigid throughout the session.]

Carl: 'It's really great, the facilities are fantastic, I'm lucky to have got a job here.'

Coach: 'I'm glad, you seem excited about the opportunities, how could I help you, do you think?'

Carl: 'Well, it's the integration software, I know it can work.'

        [Carl has repeated his technical request for help, which puzzles the coach; didn't he hear the first answer to this question?]

Coach: 'I can't help directly with that, it's not my job, but who could help?'

Carl: 'Gerry could help, but he's not here, the others think I'm stupid and wasting my time.'

> [Gerry is the research team leader who is off sick. The coach wonders if Carl needs some management support.]

Coach: 'How about John?' [Head of research and development.]

Carl: 'No.'

> [Carl looks quickly over his shoulder, stands up and holds his hand out to shake.]

Carl: 'Thank you.'

> [And walks out.]

This is a puzzling first session for the coach; it is common to have to explain what coaching is for and the differences between coaching and training and line management. The coach doesn't expect to end the first session with clear goals and areas for development, after all, coaching is imposed as part of the development programme and will not suit all participants. The coach decides to offer another one-to-one session via internal e-mail and to let the appropriate people know that Carl may need some closer management support.

Before the next one-to-one session the coach has a group session towards the end of which, Carl gets up and leaves without saying a word. One of the others says that Carl was like that at university, always a bit odd.

The coach hasn't heard back from Carl about another one-to-one session and is working when there is a knock on the door and Carl enters without waiting, carefully closes the door, then sits in the same seat as before.

Coach: 'Hello Carl, how did you think the meeting went?'

Carl: 'I needed to get on with the integration software.'

Coach: 'Most people tell me that the groups are important for management development, and enjoyable.'

Carl: 'I need to complete the software, I'm nearly there, I had to get back to work, and I'd been away for over an hour.'

> [This is an unusual response; the coach was probably expecting an apology, an urgent need to be somewhere else, a telephone call, another meeting perhaps. The coach decides to clearly challenge Carl on his behaviour.]

Coach: 'I think it was inappropriate to leave without saying anything.'

Carl: [Silence, looks away, puzzled.]

Coach: 'Do you find it difficult in groups?'

Carl: 'What's the point of them, they stop me working.'
        [The coach notes that Carl doesn't seem to make a connection between the development group and work.]

Coach: 'Isn't it part of work, talking to colleagues?'

Carl: 'Why, it's not work, is it?'
        [Something unusual is clearly going on and the coach needs to focus on this behaviour and Carl's view of others.]

Coach: 'Most people think that team work is very important.'

Carl: 'I'm not in a team, I'm developing software.'

Coach: 'Have you ever been in a team?'
        [Starting to explore Carl's past.]

Carl: 'I've never liked sports.'
        [A dead end in the questioning so the coach changes direction, whilst continuing to try to find out what is going on.]

Coach: 'When do you like to spend time with other people?'

Carl: [Looks puzzled, doesn't say anything.]

Coach: 'What about your family?'

Carl: 'They're OK, I guess.'
        [Again a very minimal answer to a question; the coach would have expected a fuller answer here.]

Coach: 'Do you have any brothers or sisters?'

Carl: 'I've got one brother, but he's very ill.'

Coach: 'I'm sorry to hear that, what's the problem?'

Carl: 'He has autistic spectrum disorder.'
        [Autism is a wide spectrum and if there is one member of the family affected the likelihood of another being affected is high. Carl was also very precise in labelling his brother's problem.]

Coach: 'That must be difficult for the family?'

Carl: 'It's not bad, I just stay in my room with the door locked.'

> [Carl's response is very functional, nothing about feelings for his brother or the emotional effects on the family. Clear pointers are starting to emerge that Carl may have some similar problems to his brother. He doesn't relate well to others and seems to see his brother's difficulties as just a practical problem. The coach needs to know if any of this has been identified in the past.]

Coach: 'Has anyone ever talked to you about this sort of thing before?'

Carl: 'No.'

Coach: 'Do you think you have a problem?'

Carl: 'I don't have a problem unless there are other people around, I don't understand what they want.'

Coach: 'Was that a problem at school?'

Carl: 'Well, they made me see the counsellor.'

Coach: 'Did that help?'

Carl: 'No.'

Coach: 'Have you seen anyone else?'

Carl: 'No.'

Coach: 'Working well with others is essential to your job here, would you be willing to have help with this?'

Carl needs a psychological assessment and, if possible, a diagnosis. The value of attaching the label of Asperger's syndrome to Carl is enormous. He will be able to accept this diagnosis, read about it, research it on the internet and at an intellectual level it will give him a greater understanding of his feelings.

From the company's point of view they will be able to harness Carl's talents. His work colleagues, with a little coaching, will be able to accommodate his behaviour. Should the coaching continue? That really depends on the coach and the amount of time available. Coaching as a secondary role to help Carl function at work may be very beneficial but Carl is likely to get more appropriate help elsewhere in the first instance.

Carl needs to talk to a specialist about his issues and the coach can encourage him in this; whether to take action, to contact a member of his family for example, without his express permission, is a difficult point in this case. Carl is not a danger to himself or others so the normal boundary of confidentiality has not been crossed. Someone with undiagnosed learning difficulties is very likely to find life easier if in the care of an appropriate professional, but is that enough of a case to break a confidentiality agreement? One course of action would be to strongly encourage Carl to ask for help, and, perhaps, to offer to make the introduction for him.

A different story

What appears as an unusual set of behaviours may have a rational explanation as in this case where old types of behaviour are no longer effective or appropriate in a new environment.

Some time after the meeting that Carl left so unusually the coach is sitting working when there is a knock at the door and Carl comes in.

Coach: 'Hello Carl, how did you think the meeting went?'

Carl: 'It was OK, I solved the problem.'

        [Again, the coach had an expectation of some sort of explanation of Carl's exit from the group, perhaps an apology.]

Coach: 'Most people tell me that the groups are important for management development and enjoyable.'

Carl: 'Well, I knew what we needed to do, I told them, and they just kept talking.'

        [This is becoming an unusual conversation; warning bells are starting to ring. Carl does not seem to see it as odd that he left a meeting without a word and did not give an explanation.]

Coach: 'The others were working out who was going to do what, how to divide tasks.'

Carl: 'I did it on my own in ten minutes, why do I need other people to help me?'

Coach: 'I thought it was a team task?'
[The coach had noted during the meeting that Carl seemed unable to pick up on non-verbal cues; not noticing how exasperated others had been when he butted in and with his answers.]

Carl: 'They were just wasting my time.'

It is clear that Carl has a completely different idea as to the purpose of the meeting, purely looking at it functionally, and his ability to solve the problem. This was not the purpose, which was a team training session. Something out of the ordinary is going on and the coach needs to explore this to get some background (the past). When Carl is questioned about his upbringing he is very open about it.

The story that unfolds is that Carl's mother brought him up alone in a small community, travelling a long distance to school. He was very intelligent, but isolated. This pattern continued, through college. The result was a well-qualified and technically brilliant person who had developed little social skills to complement his technical ability. He had found a way to relate to others through his technical brilliance, which had worked whilst the focus of his life was on academic achievement. In a way it was out of character to have applied for a position in this large company, but, again, his normal coping mechanism had worked to his advantage in that the department head had met him at a conference and helped him with the application process after being impressed with Carl's technical ability.

In this instance social skills training/coaching is likely to have enormous benefit. If Carl can accept that some of his behaviours are no longer helping him he may apply his intellect to solving the problem and find a way to work with others in a more effective way.

The issues for coaching are:

- What, if any, other support is accessible?
- Is the coaching that can be offered likely to be beneficial?
- Is coaching appropriate from the company's perspective?
- Is there any underlying psychological problem?

In a scenario such as this with the backing of a large corporation, resources are more likely to be made available to help Carl. There is very little real difference to coaching Carl than another manager who has poor interpersonal skills; there may just be more to work on. So, one of the issues to consider is whether enough time can be made available to help Carl through a lengthy process of adjustment. Group therapy could prove useful; Carl's doctor may be the best route to this.

There is nothing of substance that the coach needs to report to the sponsoring organisation – all those working with Carl will be aware of his unusual ways – but it would be important to check out that resources can be made available to help Carl for what could be a protracted process of learning about other people.

After an unusual start to coaching be aware of any other signs that appear. A referral to a doctor may be sensible at some stage to check out that there is no underlying psychological problem.

Is this real?

With a similar first session and background, in this scenario Carl walks out of the team meeting after appearing very distracted and agitated. One of his colleagues says that Carl has really changed. Others agree; apparently his work has deteriorated, he doesn't complete tasks and seems always distracted.

Carl comes into the coach's room for the one-to-one session.

Coach: 'Hello Carl, please sit down.'
Carl: [Carl cautiously sits down, looking intently at the air vent.]
Coach: 'Are you OK?'
Carl: [Nods.]
Coach: 'Why did you leave the meeting, Carl?'
         [The coach's warning bells are already ringing after the comments in the group session about Carl's change in behaviour.]

Carl: [Laughs, then says] 'I had to.'
Coach: 'Why did you have to?'
Carl: 'He told me to.'
          [Carl gets up and paces round the chair, looks intently at the air vent and then quickly over his shoulder. Clearly this is starting to appear as very strange behaviour and needs exploring.]
Coach: 'Who told you to leave?'
Carl: 'He did.'
Coach: 'I didn't hear anyone say anything.'
Carl: 'You wouldn't, he only talks to me.'
Coach: 'Who talks to you?'
          [Carl is saying that he gets instructions from 'him'; this sounds like he is hallucinating. Although Carl's behaviour has been very strange, the coach probably needs to continue asking rational questions, responding to what Carl has said 'as if' it was rational. Carl needs to be given the option of refuting his bizarre behaviour.]
Carl: [No response.]
Coach: 'Carl, what's going on?'
          [A clear request for a rational response from Carl. One possible alternative explanation to Carl's bizarre behaviour could be drug use.]
Carl: 'I don't know, they're bugging my phone.'
Coach: 'Who would want to do that?'
          [Again, a rational question from the coach – there are people who have had their phones bugged, and e-mails intercepted. There are those whose paranoia has its roots in reality.]
Carl: 'They want to, I've got secrets.'

The type of behaviour that Carl is showing is most likely a psychotic episode. The coach knows that others have noted his changing behaviour and that over two sessions Carl has shown increasingly unusual behaviour. The coach has given several opportunities to be proved wrong in assumptions of mental health problems.

There is no question that coaching will cease in a case as extreme as this. The question for the coach is how best to help Carl.

By the stage that the dialogue ends the coach has enough information to know that action will need to be taken. The questioning could continue, it may be useful to know how long Carl has been hearing voices and whether he hears voices only at work.

The key question, though, is to find out if this is totally new or if Carl has had these symptoms before and sought help. Does Carl's doctor know about this? Has Carl seen a psychiatrist or other mental health professional? If these symptoms are not new to Carl the coach has a route to appropriate help.

Someone exhibiting this sort of bizarre behaviour, talking in a clearly irrational way, is clear in their own mind of the truth of their thoughts and what is happening. The most likely outcome will be that the client would leave the session, quite normally. There is little real danger, Carl is unlikely to become threatening or violent or harm himself. It is important that the coach does not overreact. Remaining calm and collecting information so that appropriate action can be taken later is the best course of action.

The issues fall into three categories:

1 How best to help Carl?
2 What may the coach need?
3 Where are the company's needs in a situation such as this?

These categories are described further below:

1 How best to help Carl?

In the story here, the coach will have the support of a large organisation, there is likely to be a medical officer, certainly help from the human resources department and other staff. The coach may choose to leave the room, briefly, and summon assistance, returning to keep Carl company until help arrives and then handing over responsibility to someone more suitable.

In other settings the availability of help will be less. The coach may have contact information for Carl, his home telephone number for example, there may be a relative available who can offer insight into what is going on and maybe collect Carl. Carl could be happy with someone he knows around, but he may become uncomfortable, agitated, everyone is different.

Carl needs to be seen by an appropriate mental health professional promptly, but not as a medical emergency.

2 What may the coach need?

The coach needs to feel safe. Getting someone else involved and telling someone else what is happening means that the coach is not left alone to deal with a disturbed person. In a worse-case scenario, there is someone to call the police should Carl become angry or violent, or even look like harming himself. It is not part of the coaching contract to place oneself in harm's way.

Finding yourself, unexpectedly, in the company of someone who is behaving bizarrely may be frightening. Anger, threatening violence and aggression are the exception rather than the rule with someone like Carl, but the coach needs to take precautions to protect themselves and maybe others. There could be a danger of overreacting due to the bizarreness of the behaviour. If the coach knows that they have help near to hand it can help them remain calm and helpful.

The coach should take all reasonable steps to make sure that anyone who needs to know what has happened has been contacted. In an organisational setting this would include the human resources department and/or management who should then take on the responsibility of liaising with others. In other cases this may need some detective work to find a relative or close friend. It may happen that the coach is unable to do more than pass on the client to the medical system and then have to draw back, knowing only that they did all that was possible.

Whenever something this unusual happens it is good to talk. A supervisor, mentor or professional colleague can be used to discuss what happened, checking out that the coach did not miss any early signs of issues and that the action taken was professional and reasonable. Notes of the results of talking professionally about the case should be added to the coach's own session notes, which must be complete and thorough in case they need to be referred back to in the future.

3 Where are the company's needs in a situation such as this?

In a general sense Carl, the coach and the company are all best served by getting appropriate help as soon as possible. The coach may have a duty to the company in providing help with records so that the company can evidence that it has shown an appropriate duty of care to an employee.

Conclusions

These three stories about Carl have developed from a common place of someone who is technically competent and intelligent starting to behave unusually.

In the first the future is probably much happier for Carl than if he had been left to muddle through life not knowing what was going on. But, if the symptoms had not been so clear the coach may have been left thinking that Carl just didn't get on with her or him, or that Carl was one of those people who did not value the emotional side of life. Whilst this would have been a pity for Carl and his future life it would not have been dangerous or damaging psychologically although he could have found his employment prospects curtailed.

With the scenario of a person who doesn't know the social norms, much will depend on the individual's insight – do they recognise that they may have problems – and their ability to accept help and work at changing their behaviour. If nothing happened then Carl would continue as an isolated loner, with little meaningful interaction with others, probably being labelled as strange and unfriendly by those around him.

The third case, of hearing voices, may sound like nothing more than a work of fantasy, but people do have these hallucinations and they can seem to appear from nowhere. The key message is, do not panic, do not overreact, just do everything possible to ensure that the person is seen by a medical professional in a timely fashion.

Learning points

- Intelligence is not a barrier to mental health problems.
- Resistance to coaching may occasionally have its roots in mental health problems.
- Bizarre behaviour may be due to upbringing as well as mental health problems.
- With bizarre behaviour always look for a rational explanation first.
- Treatment cannot be forced on an unwilling client.
- The coach has needs as well. Don't ignore them.

8

Duncan's life in the fast lane

The story of Duncan, a 28-year-old man working in an office-based sales role, has two scenarios that develop after promotion is refused. In the first an occasional cocaine habit has started to impact more and more on work and in the second a lifelong problem of attention deficit hyperactivity disorder (ADHD) that was recognised and treated in his youth may still be giving problems in adult life and has become a barrier to promotion and more responsibility.

Duncan makes a direct approach to an independent coach. On the telephone the coach finds out that Duncan had the expectation of being given promotion to team leader but his department head had said that he wasn't ready. Duncan has been told that he needs to become more focused on the wider issues and more structured in his work to be considered as a potential team leader. The boss was openly in favour of executive coaching and sometimes talked of how much he had gained from working with a coach.

The coach found Duncan to be an appropriate coaching client and set up a contract for regular telephone sessions with occasional face-to-face meetings. Duncan sidestepped the suggestion of an initial face-to-face meeting due to diary pressure.

The coaching commences with three telephone sessions and Duncan comes over as intelligent, willing and eager to try out new behaviours at work. He reports back in a generally positive way and praises the coach for the value of the work and his hopes for promotion in the future. An opportunity arises for a face-to-face meeting and the coach pushes for this. It is for a Monday lunchtime and Duncan agrees, but without enthusiasm.

The coach telephones to check that the meeting is still OK on the Monday morning to be told that Duncan is at work, but not at his desk.

The coach has been looking forward to meeting Duncan, the telephone work has seemed to be going well and the coach hopes that a face-to-face session will enhance the coaching by building on the relationship that has formed on the telephone.

Duncan arrives ten minutes late. His appearance is not what the coach was expecting. Duncan is not the smartly dressed salesperson, but, dishevelled and unshaven, and he fails to make eye contact and reluctantly shakes hands.

The coach reviews the work they have done so far on the telephone, with little input from Duncan, who seems evasive.

So far nothing has happened to ring the warning bells, but the coach is puzzled. After getting to know someone quite well on the telephone and building up an expectation of who the client is, Duncan is not fitting this picture at all. The best the coach can think of is to wonder if Duncan has a cold or something and has only come to work so as not to miss this appointment.

Coach: 'You look as though you have had a rough week-end, have you been ill?'

Duncan: 'No, just a heavy party weekend.'

Coach: 'Do you do that a lot?'

          [Something about the difference in expect-
          ations between Duncan on the telephone and
          in reality has rung an alarm bell for the
          coach.]

Duncan: 'You've got to relax in this job.'

The rest of the face-to-face session is fairly superficial and doesn't really get anywhere.

At the next telephone session Duncan apologises for how badly the face-to-face work went and reiterates that he had had a heavy weekend and restates a desire to gain promotion with the coach's help.

However, over the next few weeks the consultations

become more erratic. On a couple of occasions Duncan is not available and on one Monday session the coach telephones to be told Duncan is off sick.

After some months of working together it is time for a formal review, which includes deciding whether to continue. The coaching will only continue if the department head agrees to sign off on payment.

When the coach raises this issue Duncan becomes quiet.

Duncan: 'I don't think the boss will agree to any more coaching.'
Coach: 'Why not, haven't things been going quite well?'
Duncan: [After a pause], 'I don't think I have achieved what they had hoped.'
Coach: 'In what way?'
Duncan: [Silence.]
Coach: 'Except for missing a couple of appointments you report meeting most goals that we have talked about.'
Duncan: [An ironic laugh.]
Coach: 'Is that not the case?'
            [There seems to be a difference between what the coach has been told about and what has actually been happening in the workplace.]
Duncan: 'Some of it.'
Coach: [Silence.]
            [Giving space rather than starting to 'interrogate' will often lead to a more truthful response.]
Duncan: 'I think the boss hoped I might change.'

Duncan then goes on to talk about the realities of his lifestyle and it becomes clear to the coach that Duncan's appearance and behaviour on the Monday of their one and only face-to-face meeting is the norm rather than the exception. The coach begins to wonder if the department head's agreement to fund coaching for Duncan was an attempt to save him from getting the sack rather than as an opportunity to gain promotion.

Duncan has become reliant on cocaine use at the weekends, initially to relax; over a period of time this has become more of a problem at work with difficulties of erratic behaviour, mood swings and a declining work performance. Initially confined to Mondays, as Duncan's recreational use of cocaine changed over time to a reliance on the drug and an addiction, he became less able to function throughout the week.

In this scenario there is nothing further to do but say goodbye. Duncan is aware that he has a problem with drug use that he has chosen, so far, not to address.

It is difficult to identify those with this type of issue when the contact is infrequent and doubly difficult if most of the communication is by telephone. Chapter 15 describes the signs and symptoms of drug and alcohol problems and knowledge of these may lead to an earlier identification of an issue. Unfortunately this is most likely to lead to the end of coaching rather than the client stopping their addictive behaviour and turning into a successful coaching client.

Most people using cocaine, or other substances including alcohol, will be aware that they have problems and can become very effective at hiding and denying the impact this is having on themselves and others. Until they are ready to accept the problem no offers of help will be successful.

In this scenario the suggestion is that Duncan's employer is aware of a problem and there would be no need for the coach to break confidentiality by informing the company. The coach may meet a client who is using drugs or alcohol where the company has no knowledge. Any decision on breaking confidentiality will need careful thought. If the coach has a formal contract with an organisation there may be a specific clause about disclosing information such as drug or alcohol problems, possibly if the job has specific requirements for sobriety or a clear head, such as driving or flying for example. The coach would then be obliged to inform the employer. A more difficult situation would occur if the coaching were private, when no third party contract would be in place. Discussions with a supervisor or experienced colleague and exploration of the issues covered in Chapter 3 will help to choose the most appropriate course of action.

A fast life leads to old distractions

Psychological issues can come and go throughout someone's life. A change in circumstances may lead to a recurrence of an old problem.

After the disappointment of not getting promotion to team leader, Duncan has a conversation with the boss who is in favour of coaching as a way for Duncan to address the issues that let him down. Duncan is popular with most of his colleagues and his boss likes him, but despairs of him ever getting the promotion he desires, as he is scatterbrained and disorganised, although competent in his sales role and always hits targets.

Duncan decides that coaching would be a worthwhile investment and makes an appointment to meet with the coach. He arrives ten minutes late and breathless from running.

Duncan: 'Sorry, sorry, I didn't notice how late it was and had to run to get here.'

Coach: 'Never mind, shall we sit? You mentioned on the phone that you wanted help to get promoted to team leader, shall we start by talking about that?'

Duncan: 'Yes of course, I've been with the company for over two years, which is a long time in sales, and really want to be a team leader . . .'

[Duncan talks about hitting targets, knowing the product and getting on with customers.]

Duncan: '. . . and the boss says she'd like to let me have the opportunity but that I'm not ready, but people have been promoted who have been there a lot less time than me.'

Coach: 'You mentioned on the phone a performance review that included areas for development, you were going to bring it today.'

Duncan: 'I know but I couldn't find it, I thought it was in the drawer, I'll have a look at home.'

Coach: 'What can you remember about the suggestions for development?'

Duncan: 'A lot of stuff about paperwork being completed on time and not being done properly . . .'

[Duncan gets up and walks around the room whilst talking.]

Duncan: '. . . and some stuff about team work and respecting others' views, I think I irritate people some of the time.'

Coach: 'What do you think you would need to be doing for the boss to consider you for team leader?'

Duncan: [Laughs and says] 'She'd probably say I need to grow up.'

This first session continues with the coach exploring what Duncan wants and the gap between where he is today and where he would need to be to be given the opportunity of team leadership. The next session is on the telephone and Duncan agrees that it would be helpful to write down in detail his goals with a view to prioritising areas for change at the start of the next session.

The coach has enjoyed the time spent with Duncan and found him likeable and keen to develop. During the session the coach had found it quite difficult to get Duncan to focus on one topic at a time; he seemed to jump around in his thoughts and conversation.

The day before the telephone session Duncan e-mails a list of goals. The coach is pleased to get this and is looking forward to the session.

This session focuses on strategies to help Duncan become more reliable with paperwork, completing reports accurately and on time, updating the customer database and making sure the boss has up-to-date information on what Duncan is doing. Duncan decides that blocking out time at the beginning and end of the day to complete these tasks without distraction would be a good way to achieve this.

The coach and Duncan are talking about how this has worked in the next session:

Duncan: 'It's sort of worked, I'm getting better, but I keep getting distracted, the phone rings or someone wants to talk.'

Coach: 'That sounds like a good start.'

Duncan: 'I know but that's the least of my problems at the moment. I'm in big trouble after a meeting, I interrupted the sales director, the boss was really cross afterwards as I wasn't supposed to be there really, she'd asked me to go to see what happens at managers' meetings.'

Coach: 'What happened?'

Duncan: 'I jumped to conclusions about what he was saying without listening, he was very sarcastic.'

Coach: 'Well, we can't wind the clock back on that.'

Duncan: 'I'm always doing things like that.'

Coach: 'What happens?'

Duncan: 'I just need to think before opening my mouth sometimes.'

Coach: [Silence.]

Duncan: 'I'll never get promotion, no one will ever trust me now, it's pointless trying.'

            [This meeting has had an effect on Duncan and has depressed him but he pulls himself together and continues with the coaching session.]

Duncan: 'Never mind, as you say, it can't be helped, I am getting somewhere on doing my paperwork.'

There have been a lot of clues so far to store in the corner that indicate that things may not be what they seem for Duncan in this scenario:

- A generally forgetful and disorganised way of working.
- Restlessness.
- Impulsive behaviour.
- Mood changes, up one minute and depressed the next.

These are hints that some sort of psychological problem may be involved rather than clear evidence. So far the most likely 'guess' would be an immature personality as suggested by the boss in the first session, 'She'd probably say I need to grow up.'

    Without some clear indication from the client it is unlikely that any coach would pick up on childhood ADHD as a detailed psychological history would be needed to confirm this.

Part way through the next session, which is face to face, Duncan starts to talk about more difficulties:

Duncan: 'I think the boss is right, that I'm not ready for management yet. If I try to be organised and keep the records up to date I don't get the sales I need. I'm going to struggle to hit target this month the way things are going, that hasn't happened for ages.'

Coach: 'Are you saying that being more organised makes selling harder?'

Duncan: 'It's as though I can do one or the other, but not both.'

Coach: 'Is it a time issue?'

Duncan: 'I don't think so, I don't seem able to switch from selling to being organised and doing the detail stuff and then back again.'

Coach: 'That sounds difficult.'

Duncan: 'Difficult! Work hasn't been this hard since the first couple of months when I had just started.'

Coach: 'What was that like?'
        [A link to an historically similar period can give clues as to what is going on now.]

Duncan: 'Really hard work, I thought I couldn't do it; there was so much to learn, all the processes, all the products. I think they were close to letting me go when it all fell into place.'

Coach: 'How did things fall into place?'
        [The coach has some suspicions that Duncan may be struggling with more than learning new behaviours and wants to know about this early period of work.]

Duncan: 'I just kept going, put in the hours, it was hard work and depressing sometimes but I was really enjoying the buzz, it all worked out in the end.'
        [There is nothing in this reply to suggest a psychological issue.]

Coach: 'Is that what's needed now? Trying to change the way you work can be difficult at times and even seem impossible.'

[Is there an expectation that developing new work practices will be straightforward and easy? The coach is thinking that support may be needed to help Duncan stay motivated and keep going until 'It all falls into place.']

Duncan: 'Learning new stuff has always been hard work.'

Coach: 'But you succeed, I've seen your CV and achievements.'

Duncan: 'I thought I'd got past all that and left it behind me.'

[An unusual comment and the first real clue to some long-term problems.]

Coach: 'Left all what behind?'

[Focusing clearly for the first time on a potential issue.]

Duncan: 'School was really difficult, I was called a problem child, disruptive, I wanted to learn but couldn't concentrate.'

[It sounds like Duncan has had similar problems at school, in the first few months of his present job and now, with new things to learn.]

Coach: 'How did you cope with that?'

[What worked in the past? Suspicions are being confirmed that Duncan has some specific learning problems that have occurred at several points in his life.]

Duncan: 'They gave me tablets.'

Coach: 'Did they help?'

Duncan: 'Oh yes, once I'd got the tablets I could concentrate, but the doctor stopped them when I was at college, they were for children and I didn't need them anymore.'

Coach: 'Do you wish you had them now?'

[A way of exploring similarities between Duncan's present problems and his schooling difficulties.]

Duncan: 'Well, they certainly made school a lot easier.'

Coach: 'Did your childhood doctor use any names to describe the problems you had?'

Duncan: 'I had an attention disorder, or something, there was a long name for it I know.'

Coach: 'Attention deficit hyperactivity disorder?'

Duncan: 'That's it! But I thought only children got that?'

Coach: 'I don't know, but you seem to be saying that there are a lot of similarities between your struggles at work now and your struggles at school. Would it be worth seeing your doctor do you think?'

There are many possible 'illnesses' that can recur later in life. Until Duncan mentioned tablets and attention disorder all the coach knew was that he had seen a doctor as a child about some school problems. The way forward would be similar, a suggestion to visit his doctor.

This is one of the examples of mental illnesses where the medical profession has different views (see Chapter 16) and some doctors will decide to stop medication once the child has become an adult, whilst others may continue with the prescription of stimulant substances into adulthood. It may be that Duncan had been told to come back to the doctor if his problems recurred, but had either forgotten this or not made the link between childhood problems and his workplace difficulties.

In any client a recurrence of a previous mental illness is best dealt with by suggesting a visit to the doctor. The doctor will be in a position to decide if this is something similar to before or something new.

If Duncan visits a doctor who decides that further stimulant medication is needed then coaching is likely to become much easier and very helpful for him, once the medication has taken effect. Should the doctor choose not to prescribe medication then the decision must lie with Duncan to decide whether to seek a second opinion. Without medication coaching may still prove very useful for Duncan as he struggles on to find ways to cope with his attention problems, disorganisation, restlessness and impulsivity at work.

There is no need to inform the company, although Duncan may choose to tell colleagues in the future, and no need to change the coaching.

Conclusions

Two very different issues have been illustrated here but with many superficial similarities of erratic and unreliable behaviour, difficulty in attention to detail and mood swings.

In the first scenario the coach would have remained unaware of the cocaine habit unless the client had talked about it. There are many situations where the most attentive and knowledgeable coach would not identify signs of mental health problems unless the client talked of them as contact is infrequent and the coach does not usually see the client 'working' in their normal environment. The coach relies on the client being truthful and it is easy for someone to hide their 'secrets' and maintain a veneer of effectiveness.

In the second scenario Duncan was not trying to hide anything and had a genuine desire to get promoted, life just seemed to get in the way. His behaviour was sabotaging his intentions at work; in a way he was his only barrier to promotion. There are many people who have a personality that seems to get in the way of what they want to achieve. Some of these will have mental health issues that need treatment, or may benefit from therapy, others may choose to adapt to their personality by finding an environment to live and work in that suits them. A structured job, without too much responsibility, would suit an adult with ADHD, where they knew what to do and could cope with the day-to-day activities.

Learning points
- Mental health problems can become a barrier to progress in life.
- Coaching may be inappropriately suggested as a solution.
- Coaching may highlight or expose the problems.
- A client may choose to hide the problems.
- A client may not recognise the problems.
- The responsibility to address issues lies with the client.

9

Elizabeth's stressful life

A life of trying to be all things to all people leaves Elizabeth with problems that she cannot cope with, and the coach has problems too.

Elizabeth has been on a training course for three days and found it very challenging, both from the work perspective and being away from home. In conversation with one of the trainers the subject of life and personal coaching comes up and Elizabeth decides that it could be helpful for her. Shortly afterwards she contacts a coach and arranges a series of sessions.

Before meeting for the first time the coach has found out that Elizabeth is 38, married with three children and that she is an assistant editor at a publishing company which encourages flexible working including working from home for part of each week.

In the first session the coach and client explore what Elizabeth hopes to achieve. She has a good education and hoped of a bright future in publishing but isn't getting on as well as she had expected. Her children are 7, 5 and 3 years of age and before they were born she was doing well. She wants to move on from what she regards as a job that is going nowhere and asks the coach to facilitate her career development. They discuss goal setting and the coach asks Elizabeth to rewrite her CV for the next session as a prelude to applying for a new job.

Elizabeth arrives ten minutes late for the second session, flustered and harassed.

Elizabeth: 'Sorry, sorry, Alice isn't well. I had to take her to the doctors, there was no one else who could do it.'

Coach: 'Never mind. Have you remembered to bring your CV?'

Elizabeth: 'Damn, I forgot it, how stupid is that.'

The session proceeds as expected, exploring Elizabeth's life and priorities and the coach begins to get the picture of a woman with a busy life and little support. Little active coaching takes place, it is as though Elizabeth cannot see any answers or is looking for 'expert' advice to solve her problems.

On the third session Elizabeth still hasn't produced the CV and confesses that she hasn't written it.

Coach: 'Have I misunderstood? Sorry, I thought you'd done the CV and forgotten to bring it.'

Elizabeth: 'There's too much pressure, I'm tired all the time, I don't sleep well. Everyone wants a chunk of me. My Dad's in hospital, it's not serious but Mum expects me to drive her there every day.'
[Elizabeth starts to cry.]
          [There have been many signs that Elizabeth is struggling with everything she has in her life at present and the coach starts to fill in the background.]

Coach: 'How long has it been like this?'

Elizabeth: 'Oh I don't know, it feels like forever . . . probably since the baby was born.'
          [Exploring the past, the coach is trying to find out whether Elizabeth has always felt stressed or if it is just that a family, a job and a demanding mother is too much at the moment.]

Coach: 'So it was all right before that was it?'

Elizabeth: 'It was hard work but I could cope, I should never have had Alice.'
          [By now it's becoming clear to the coach that trying to help Elizabeth refocus and rebalance her career will not suffice. The picture

that has emerged is of someone whose expectations of what she can achieve are unrealistic, she has too much to do.]

Coach: 'You originally asked for help to find a more satisfying job, is that still what you want?'

Elizabeth: 'I can't cope with this one, I suppose I thought a new job would be a new start.'

Coach: 'Elizabeth, I'm wondering whether you feel you are coping at the moment?'

[Widening the questioning to find out how pervasive these feelings of life being too much are for Elizabeth.]

Elizabeth: 'The best time is when I am in the office, working, and all I have to do is my job, no one else can get to me, someone else is looking after the children, I can't see all the housework that I should have done and my mother can't phone. It's ironic that the least stressful time is when I'm working.'

Coach: 'I suppose there is some logic in looking for a better job, when work sounds like it is where you can relax at the moment.'

Elizabeth: 'But a new job, probably full time and they wouldn't be as easy going when I need time off, is going to be too much for me isn't it?'

Coach: 'I don't know, it might be, it would probably be stressful for a time.'

Elizabeth: 'That I can do without, I'm exhausted most of the time as it is.'

Coach: 'What can you do?'
[Is there any plan?]

Elizabeth: 'Just keep going I suppose, it will get easier when Alice goes to school.'

[A plan of sorts, but not one that sounds likely to help Elizabeth rebalance her life in the short term.]

Coach: 'You talk of being tired and exhausted quite a lot, have you seen a doctor recently?'

[There are no signs of mental health problems, just stress and tiredness due to a very busy life. The coach needs to try to work out a plan. This is the third session and no 'coaching' has really taken place yet. Elizabeth has no ideas except to keep going. Seeing a doctor would check for any physical problems and give the opportunity for a psychological assessment.]

Elizabeth: 'I seem to spend half my life at the doctor's, but not for me. Why, do you think I'm ill, what do you mean?'

Coach: 'I don't think I mean anything in particular, just that it might be a sensible precaution.'

At the fourth session Elizabeth is much calmer. She reports that she has been to the doctor, had a check-up and a few blood tests and that there is nothing wrong with her physically. The doctor suggested that she might be doing too much and couldn't be 'super woman'.

Elizabeth has demonstrated a clear stress-related problem and is in an ideal situation with her life coach to set priorities and improve her life. Intelligent high achievers are at risk of burnout, adding more and more into their lives until something happens that forces a change.

A conversation with Elizabeth about changing the scope of the coaching and likely outcomes would be appropriate before starting to work with her on her life in a more holistic fashion. However stressed Elizabeth may be she may choose to stop the coaching rather than look at what may be difficult choices in her life.

The coach would need to look out for any deterioration in Elizabeth, any signs of psychological problems and barriers to coaching. For example, helping Elizabeth build more appropriate boundaries with her mother, so that Elizabeth is not always available, sounds reasonable and helpful. But, if this did not work because Elizabeth struggles to make or keep new rules about being available for her mother then therapy may be indicated if she wishes to change this type of behaviour.

What may have happened in this scenario is that Elizabeth has experienced being really listened to in a way that has allowed her to face how difficult her life has become for the first time in a realistic way. This type of opening up, with the possibility of a 'can of worms' appearing, may often take a little while to settle before the coach is in a position to constructively evaluate whether coaching is likely to be helpful or whether the client would be best served by seeing someone else.

But, something unusual could have happened.

Is this really so strange?

Deciding that there is a serious mental health issue without questioning in depth can lead to inappropriate actions by the coach, as happens in this scenario.

Elizabeth meets the coach for the first time, her priority is to revitalise her career as she thinks that this will lead to a far more satisfying life in general. The coach finishes the session with the impression of someone who is unrealistic in their expectations, not just of how coaching can help, but of life in general. Elizabeth seems to want everything to be perfect in her life.

In the second session Elizabeth becomes quite tearful:

Elizabeth: 'There's too much pressure, I'm tired all the time, I don't sleep well. Everyone wants a chunk of me. It's like there's a voice there all the time going Elizabeth do this, Elizabeth do that.'
             [The coach interprets this as hearing voices and is concerned.]
Coach: 'How long has it been like this?'
Elizabeth: 'Forever, . . . since the baby was born.'
Coach: 'Which baby is that?'
Elizabeth: 'Alice, the three-year-old, she gets on my nerves, cries all the time, not like the others. It's as though she's possessed and knows just how to control me.'
Coach: 'Have you done anything about it?'
Elizabeth: 'No there's nothing to do, I wish I didn't have her.'
             [Alarm bells are ringing, the coach remembers Elizabeth's anger after the wasted journey to the doctors with Alice, when there was nothing wrong and she had said 'I could

have throttled her'. The coach has 'stored in the corner' that Elizabeth thinks her daughter is possessed, is controlling her in some way and that Elizabeth has talked of hearing voices. The coach is concerned she may be psychotic, and decides to challenge Elizabeth on these concerns.]

Coach: 'You don't really mean that?'

Elizabeth: 'You know, sometimes I do.'

             [Confirmation for the coach that Elizabeth intends to harm her daughter.]

Coach: 'I'm really concerned about what you are saying, Elizabeth, I need to phone your husband to let him know that you shouldn't be left alone with your children. I think we should go to your doctors now; I've got the car outside.'

However implausible the above dialogue may appear, the coach has responded to the words being said. Elizabeth stated that she hears voices that command her to do things, a sign of hallucination, that she is struggling with her daughter and wishes she didn't have her and when challenged restates this wish, an intention to harm another. But, the coach has listened to the words and not what is being said. The coach has reacted to the words being used in an overly simplistic and suspicious way and not viewed Elizabeth holistically or taken the time to check out the meaning or give Elizabeth the opportunity to refute these suspicions.

In this case it sounds likely that the stress that Elizabeth is under due to so many pressures and people calling on her time has not been recognised by those around her and that Elizabeth has found that the only way to be noticed is to shout or threaten. When she is with someone who is able to listen she reacts by talking in the way that she has found works, sometimes, with those who do not routinely listen and acknowledge her feelings and uses strong, exaggerated language. When someone who is taken advantage of by others finally has an opportunity to talk about it they are quite likely to be very angry, and, of course, it is safe to be angry with the coach.

There are similar opportunities for miscommunication when anyone feels safe enough, or threatened enough, to vent strong feelings. The coach may feel threatened, when no threat is intended, or appalled when someone talks about something or suggests an action that is in opposition to the coach's value system. Particular care should be taken to check and double check any suspicions when communication could be impaired by cultural differences. This could be age-related differences in language, gender-related or cross-cultural issues when working with someone from a different ethnic background.

Clients need listening to and looking at holistically, not at attitudes and intentions in isolation, and empathically, from their viewpoint and frame of reference and care should be taken not to jump to inappropriate conclusions before checking out meaning.

Who is the coach listening to?

From a similar start, things take a different direction in this next scenario.

In the third session Elizabeth becomes quite tearful:

Elizabeth: 'There's too much pressure, I'm tired all the time, I don't sleep well. In fact I really look forward to a glass of wine in the evening, it helps me sleep.'

Coach: 'Is this affecting you?'
         [Is what affecting her, the pressure, the tiredness, the lack of sleep or the glass of wine?]

Elizabeth: 'Waking up and getting going in the morning is really difficult, I don't know how I'll manage if I get that new job.'
         [In reality Alice, the youngest child, is still waking every night, but the coach 'hears' Elizabeth say that she has a hangover in the morning.]

Coach: 'How long have you been drinking like this?'

Elizabeth: [slightly surprised] 'Oh, I don't know, the last year or two I suppose.'

> [After all, the coach must have a reason for
> asking such a question.]

Coach: 'Do you feel guilty about it?'
Elizabeth: 'Guilty? About what?'
Coach: 'Your drinking.'
Elizabeth: 'Why should I, my husband drinks far more than
            I do, it's not as if I get drunk every night.'
Coach: 'Don't you think you should stop?'
Elizabeth: 'Whatever for, it's not a problem.'
Coach: 'Continuing to abuse alcohol like you are will
            put your children at risk and no one will employ
            you.'
Elizabeth: 'I don't believe I'm hearing this.'
Coach: 'People often find the truth hard to hear.'

The truth that is hard to hear in this situation is that the coach has completely misread what is being said. There is a lack of reality throughout this conversation; it is as though the coach is talking to someone else. The coach has jumped to the conclusion that enjoying a glass of wine means that Elizabeth has an alcohol problem and a hangover every morning. It may well be that the coach has made this connection due to their own past, some relationship that involved inappropriate drinking for example has unconsciously impacted on the conversation today. This is known as countertransference, from the psychodynamic viewpoint, and, simplistically, is a confusion over 'my stuff – your stuff' where the coach is thinking, feeling or having a conversation that is not based in the reality of what is happening, but on some historical part of the coach's life that has become mixed up with the present conversation.

If the coach thinks they are seeing signs of mental health problems it is important to check these out before taking action. One part of this checking is an examination of the coach's personal, internal, relationship with the possible problem. In some cases the possible link will be quite obvious. If the coach has experience of alcohol problems they may be more likely to spot possible signs of alcohol abuse than someone who has little awareness or experience of this. Similarly, the parent or sibling of someone with autism may 'see' signs of autism in others that are of little relevance; after all, everyone sits on the autistic spectrum somewhere. This idea of countertransference can be more of an issue when the reason for the coach's misreading of the situation is hidden; it unconsciously impacts on how the coach behaves. The client may remind the coach of someone from their past, a parent for example (there doesn't have to be a physical resemblance, it could be a phrase, a mannerism or a tone of voice), and the coach acts 'as if' they were talking to that person.

In this scenario of Elizabeth and a glass of wine, it could be that the coach's sister had a problem with alcohol and the coach was powerless to help or even that the coach grew up with an alcoholic mother. Supervision is an important check that the coach is dealing with the client and not some imaginary other from the past.

The trouble with talking

In this final scenario, Elizabeth becomes quite tearful in the third session and the dialogue is as follows:

Elizabeth: 'There's too much pressure, I'm tired all the time, I don't sleep well. Everyone wants a chunk of me. I cannot go on like this.'

[The coach remembers back to an earlier session when Elizabeth had talked of not finding work as interesting now as she used to and now said that she couldn't continue. Warning bells start to ring – is Elizabeth severely depressed?]

Coach: 'Like what?'

Elizabeth: 'Oh, you know, no one appreciates what I do, they hardly notice when I'm there.'

[The coach is getting a little confused; Elizabeth is talking depressed but is quite active in her speech. Her general manner is more angry than depressed.]

Coach: 'Who hardly notices?'

['Who do you want to notice you?' would have given Elizabeth the opportunity to say whom she was angry with for not noticing. 'Who hardly notices?' is an open question and Elizabeth gives an expansive, emotional response, which does not help the coach gather more information.]

Elizabeth: 'Everyone, if the work was done no one would notice if I wasn't there.'

Coach: 'It sounds like you are saying you are invisible.' [This line of questioning is moving towards the therapeutic way of working, but is the coach thinking that Elizabeth is depressed, because her words suggest this, and has missed that she is acting more angry than depressed?]

Elizabeth: 'Absolutely!'

Coach: 'What can we do about it?'

Elizabeth: 'The reason I'm here is that I cannot continue.'

After the session the coach is puzzled by Elizabeth's low mood and depressive manner, but it is only in parts of the session. There have been times when Elizabeth is positive and actively engaging in the coaching, looking at steps that can be taken and making plans for change. The two phrases, 'I cannot go on like this' and 'I cannot continue' keep coming back to the coach who decides to discuss it in group supervision.

This discussion quickly moves from looking at the case to a general discussion of suicide, with one member of the group monopolising the conversation with strong views about the dangers of suicide in a client. At the end this person challenges the coach to take action, 'What are you going to do, you can't ignore suicidal intentions.'

This leaves the coach more puzzled than before and with the worry that something must be done or Elizabeth may commit suicide.

What would you do? Some options would be:

1 Do nothing, wait for the next session.
2 Contact Elizabeth and try to have a conversation on the telephone to check she is all right.
3 Contact Elizabeth and let her know of the concerns that she may be depressed and contemplating suicide.

4 Contact a member of her family, or even the emergency services, and tell them of her suicidal thoughts.

Looking at the whole process may help with the choice of what to do. Elizabeth is under a lot of pressure just to get through her normal day-to-day routine and she has approached a coach as a way to find a more satisfying life. She shows a whole range of strong emotions from tearfulness and emotive language to anger, but she actively engages in the coaching at other times. The coach may have been instrumental in bringing to the surface some of the emotionally charged statements that Elizabeth has made by following a more therapeutic style of questioning. Holistically there is nothing to suggest that Elizabeth is suicidal, or even severely depressed and the coach has chosen a good course of action in discussing the puzzling moods in supervision. Unfortunately the supervision process is highjacked by another coach who appears to have their own agenda to follow, rather than focusing on the case in question, and ends with a challenge that clients with suicidal intentions cannot be ignored. This is reasonable, good practice, but the other coach has not been thinking about Elizabeth but clients with suicidal ideas in general.

What this scenario does suggest is that Elizabeth has potential mental health issues at the moment; she seems to be very stressed. The dialogue may be pointing to a diagnosis of mixed anxiety with depression (see Chapter 13) or possibly a personality disorder. Elizabeth is showing signs that suggest either an impulsive or a histrionic personality type (Chapter 17). With this in mind the best course of action for the coach is to wait until the next planned session, choice 1 above.

This final scenario is very similar to the first, where the coaching could appropriately continue, but Elizabeth is showing higher stress levels and, possibly, less emotional control. This is a borderline case between coaching and therapy and the best way forward would depend on Elizabeth's views, the experience of the coach, what other options are available locally and the specifics of any future coaching contract such as frequency of sessions.

Conclusions

The core of these four scenarios is that Elizabeth is doing too much and is very stressed. A client such as Elizabeth is likely to have more serious problems in the future if she is unable to take action to restructure her life.

Coaching is likely to help, as outlined in the first and fourth scenario, but the coach needs to be aware that there could be an underlying psychological problem that prevents Elizabeth from making sensible changes to her life. If coaching does not show benefits fairly quickly then the coach should consider suggesting a more therapeutic relationship as a way of helping her.

The key to the second and third scenarios is to ensure that any reaction to a sign of mental illness is based on clear evidence and not just an isolated sentence. Look at the client holistically, as a whole person, and take action based on this.

Learning points

- Listen to the client.
- Look at the client.
- Respond to the client.
- A person's normal way of behaving can suggest a psychological issue.
- A highly emotional person is not mentally ill.
- In discussions with a supervisor or others check that any suggestions make sense for your client.

10

Frances has no place to hide

A history of abuse and an eating disorder lead to difficulties with coaching as Frances tries to hide these problems from the coach, and her work colleagues.

Frances has recently been promoted to a new role that involves working far more closely with colleagues. She used to work in a small team that was task focused and insular. The new environment means collaborating in large teams and meeting with clients. The new office culture is friendly, gregarious and fast paced. Desks are shared on an as-needed basis in a large open-plan office. Work often continues in the canteen and coffee shop. After a couple of months the line manager suggests some coaching for Frances as she is struggling. Coaching is seen as a positive in the organisation and is routinely offered during times of change and as support to help employees achieve their best. The company agrees to pay for three months' coaching and gives Frances a list of authorised coaches to contact.

After making a couple of telephone calls, Frances chooses a female coach from the list. Frances meets the coach for the first time as arranged and the coach notices a well-groomed and expensively dressed young woman who seems confident and assured.

Coach: 'What is it we're going to try to achieve?'
Frances: 'I'm struggling after promotion, it's so different.'
Coach: 'What sorts of things are different?'
Frances: 'It used to be easy, we were all girls together, I could have a laugh, there was no pressure and I just got on with my work.'

Coach: 'And now?'
Frances: 'There's so much pressure, there's so many people and they all want something from me.'
Coach: 'What do they want?'
            [Frances is visibly becoming agitated and upset. The coach changes direction and they spend time talking about goals and what needs to happen. It sounds like one of the issues is that Frances is not clear how to work day to day in the new environment. The coach asks if there is a person who Frances could approach for support and advice, in a mentoring role, to help her settle in.]
Frances: [Frances looks uncomfortable about the thought of asking someone for help.]
Coach: 'It sounds like a best friend in the office could really help you settle in.'
Frances: 'There's no one there I could ask.'
Coach: 'Would you see it as some sort of failure, asking for support?'
Frances: 'No, no, not at all, it's just who to ask.'

At the end of the first session one of the tasks is for Frances to find a mentor, a friend in the office to talk to about day-to-day work processes.

A telephone session follows:

Coach: 'Who have you found to help with day-to-day questions?'
Frances: 'No one, I asked Judy, but she said no, but it was a great idea and that I should speak to Roger or Peter.'
Coach: 'And what did they say?'
Frances: 'I didn't ask.'
Coach: 'That's a pity, when will you be able to speak to them?'
Frances: [Silence.]
Coach: 'Frances, are you still there?'
Frances: 'Oh yes, I just find it hard to talk like this on the phone.'

Frances and the coach agree to the next session face to face. This telephone session has been difficult and the coach has felt she was talking to a very different person. Face to face Frances was able to engage in the coaching, although she seemed quite fragile, emotionally, some of the time. On the telephone she seemed very distant and careful in her responses, as though she were looking for the correct response rather than a truthful one.

The coach has realised after these first two sessions that Frances has some fragile areas and that she needs to be more cautious.

Part way through the next session Frances seems to be struggling with any idea of looking for ways to achieve and enjoy the new role:

Coach: 'This new role seems very different to what you were used to, you seem really unhappy with it.'
Frances: 'It's not the job, it's the people.'
Coach: 'Are they not friendly?'
Frances: 'They're too friendly, I'm not used to that. I wish they'd leave me alone to get on with my job.'
Coach: 'Is it anyone in particular?'
            [The coach has thoughts of sexual harassment.]
Frances: 'No, it's everyone.'
Coach: 'You mentioned liking Judy.'
Frances: 'She's lovely, she's the only one I can talk to, but I don't have to work with her very much.'
Coach: 'Who is giving you problems at work, Frances?'
            [Direct questioning to understand what is going on is sometimes needed when the client's responses seem at odds. Frances has said 'it's everyone', and then how nice one person is. Clearly Frances is having problems with some of her work colleagues and coaching will struggle without some clarity around what is really happening.]
Frances: [Tearfully] 'It's men.'

Frances goes on to talk of having been abused in the past and any intimacy with men leads to severe anxiety and panic. The new office environment, although ideal for most, is an impossible environment for Frances to work in.

For Frances the move to a large office where daily contact and a close working relationship with a variety of men is expected has led to frequent reminders of her past abuse and an inability to function as is expected of her or as she used to in the much safer environment of her previous role.

The difficult telephone session may have been due to Frances not having the visual reminder that she was talking to a woman and becoming unconsciously confused, thinking she needed to respond as if her coach was a man for safety.

This type of issue is a significant barrier to any coaching and continuing is unlikely to be of benefit.

The company does not need to be told of any of Frances' issues, any disclosure is for her to decide on in the future. Continuing with the coaching contract to the end is unlikely to be helpful. It would remove the need for either the coach or Frances to explain why it had stopped early, but, Frances' behaviour in the office and ability to work effectively will not change unless she can resolve her abusive history in her own mind and so it is unlikely that the coaching will be evaluated positively.

The coach may be able to help Frances by asking if she has ever talked to anyone about this. Frances may not know that she can get help and may have thought that she must avoid difficult situations and working with men in particular. She may have felt that she had got over her past problems only to find that the more stressful office environment brought a return of her anxiety and panic. The coach can try to aid Frances in finding the type of help she needs.

It may be helpful to think of reactions to specific situations such as this as PTSD (post traumatic stress disorder) and treatment is specialised. A family doctor may have access to suitable treatment or be able to suggest where to go. There are specialist groups available in some areas that can help adult survivors of sexual abuse.

Adults who have been abused in any way earlier in their life will often have found ways to work around the problem area and relationships by avoiding them, defending against them and developing strategies that avoid stressful situations. There will be situations where coaching can continue, effectively and ethically, by focusing on other parts of the client's life. But trying to coach in the area of the past traumatic experience will be ineffective and could be very damaging for the client.

Let's have lunch?

Sometimes seemingly trivial comments can lead to the disclosure of issues. In this scenario, Frances avoids talking about a potentially serious problem throughout a successful course of coaching.

During the first session Frances tells the coach that her manager wants her to become more involved with the rest of the team, sharing tasks, collaborating and developing ideas collectively as this is the culture of the team and seen as the key factor in its success. Frances is seen as a technically competent employee and reliable who needs to become more involved on a day-to-day basis to achieve her potential.

There is a team lunch once a month that is seen as very important and attendance is expected. Frances has not yet been to one. One task that results from the first session is to attend the next team lunch.

Coach:	'Last time we spoke, a task was to go to this lunch.'
Frances:	'I know, but, it was impossible, there was so much to do.'
Coach:	'You said that going to the lunch was expected of everyone? I thought that one of your goals was to make sure you got to the next team lunch?'
Frances:	'Well, it was, but I couldn't help it.'
Coach:	'What stopped you going?'
Frances:	[Silence.]
Coach:	'Frances, I'm trying to understand what got in the way of going to the team lunch.'
Frances:	'You can't understand.'
Coach:	'What can't I understand?'
Frances:	'Look this is no big deal, it's more important that I have collaborated with Mark and Steph on the project bid, that's gone really well.'

The session continues with some good coaching around collaboration and task divisions in a team.

The coach has the idea that Frances would benefit from coaching around the informal working that is very much the culture of the team. Frances appears very task focused and whilst this is important she misses out on the informal opportunities, networking and dynamics.

Several more sessions follow with good progress being made. Frances seems more aware of the informal team working and able to become actively involved. She seems much more relaxed about the new ways of working and the coach is pleased with progress made. There has been no repeat of the earlier outburst when Frances was questioned on the team lunch. Frances was unable to go to the next monthly lunch as she was off sick for a couple of days, missing a client meeting as well.

Frances arrives on a glorious early summer's day at the coach's office for the last session, wearing a long baggy jacket:

Coach: 'Hello Frances, shall I take your coat?'
Frances: 'No thanks, I'll keep it on, it's quite chilly in here.'
Coach: 'As this is our last session let's review where we've been, what goals were set and how they have been achieved.'
Frances: 'It's been great, hasn't it, I've managed so much more over the last couple of months and everyone is really pleased with my work now.'
           [Frances has taken control of the session and maintains this until towards the end when the coach brings in the remaining goal that has not been covered, not thinking much of it.]
Coach: 'Which only leaves the team lunch once a month, it's a shame you couldn't go as you would have met all your goals then.'
           [The coach is speaking fairly lightheartedly on this, but gets an unexpected response from Frances.]
Frances: 'You just don't understand, do you?'
Coach: 'What don't I understand?'

Frances: 'I don't eat with other people.'
Coach: 'What, ever?!'
Frances: [No reply.]

Chapter 18 looks in detail at eating disorders. The prevalence of this condition makes it one of the issues that coaches may well come across. In this scenario Frances was able to avoid her problems impacting on work for some time, by concealing her 'thinness' with bulky clothing and avoiding social eating situations. She is likely to have been able to maintain this status quo until forced to acknowledge it due to medical problems.

Within the context of the coaching she was able to distract the coach from her refusal to eat in public with sensible excuses at first and by maintaining control of the sessions by talking about other issues (than the team lunch). It is quite likely that a client with this type of eating disorder would have maintained secrecy about it through this last session, just by joining in the lighthearted approach of the coach and agreeing that she would make an extra effort to get to the next team lunch, continuing to avoid this in the workplace as long as possible.

A slightly startled 'What, ever?!' from the coach was a response to what was thought to be a lighthearted ending to a successful coaching contract that changed due to Frances' angry reply of 'I don't eat with other people' and needs following through. One way would be to apologise and continue to a normal ending with something like 'I'm sorry, I seemed to have intruded on a private area', which allows Frances to maintain her defence and hide her eating disorder. Direct questioning about this disclosure of a psychological problem is beyond the coaching contract and apologising and then leaving this alone is an appropriate response in many cases.

Another way to continue would be cautious questioning to see how aware Frances is of the problem with a view to deciding if any further action is necessary. PPP questioning (Chapter 2) will give more information and can be particularly helpful for the client, if they have not talked to anyone about problems before.

Coach: 'Have I touched on a sensitive area?'
Frances: 'Yes, I'm sorry I was angry, it's not your fault, I don't talk about it.'
Coach: 'I'm sorry; I wasn't thinking anything about it really. How long have you avoided eating with other people?'
            [The past.]
Frances: 'Since university.'
Coach: 'Is it everyone?'
            [How pervasive?]
Frances: 'I just keep myself to myself and no one notices usually.'
            [Not a direct answer but a suggestion that Frances is aware of the problem and that she is hiding it from those around her.]
Coach: 'It's being noticed now. How long can you avoid the team lunches without comments?'
            [How does Frances plan to maintain her secrecy about eating with the pressure to go to team lunches?]
Frances: 'I don't know, I suppose I just hoped no one would notice.'
Coach: 'Have you ever talked to anyone about this?'
Frances: 'No.'
Coach: 'I wonder if you should? I know it's not really my place to intrude but I am concerned that you have an eating disorder.'
Frances: 'I know I have, but it's OK, I'm alright really.'
Coach: 'It might be best to talk to your doctor about it, you could get really ill if you continue.'
Frances: 'I don't like him, can I continue to see you, I'll pay.'
            [An attempt to continue to hide the issue perhaps, but also confusion between the role of a coach and a therapist by the client.]
Coach: 'I'm not trained to help with things like this. A doctor would be the best person to talk to first, they would know.'
Frances: 'OK, but can I still see you as well. You've been so helpful and you understand. I don't want to have to tell someone I don't know all about it.'

Coach: 'What about friends and family?'
           [Frances is trying to persuade the coach to
           continue the relationship, even though this
           is the last session and the coach has stated
           that she is not trained to help. The coach is
           asking what other support may be available.]
Frances: 'There's no one, really.'

Frances is pushing the boundaries of the coaching relationship and the coach is in a potentially difficult situation.

An eating disorder is life threatening and Frances needs
to seek medical help. She may go to see her doctor; equally
likely she may ignore the warning and continue as normal.
At this stage it would be difficult to justify a case for breaking confidentiality and informing others of the suspicions;
the only contact the coach has is with the company and
nothing that Frances has said indicates a need for her
employer to be informed.

The discussions in Chapter 4 about stopping coaching
and offering support whilst the client finds help highlight
the issues should the coach decide to maintain contact
with Frances after coaching has ended. Arguably there is a
case for the coach maintaining some supportive contact with
Frances whilst she waits for a referral to an appropriate professional. She says she has no close friends and family to talk
to and the issue has been exposed as a direct result of coaching. Any contact would need to be cautious and very focused
on the goal of Frances finding specialist help.

Conclusions

In several ways these two scenarios are similar. Frances has
an area of her life that she is aware of and is experienced in
avoiding. With the first scenario, the issue of difficulties
around men and the anxiety this provokes, she has been able
to lead an outwardly successful working life by avoiding
close contact with men wherever possible. With the second
scenario of an eating disorder she is adept at avoiding
any situation where she may be expected to eat in front of
others.

Neither scenario is likely to respond to coaching, something more therapeutic is needed. Both issues present a solid barrier to coaching. Progress can be made in other areas but Frances will continue to struggle in this new working environment until the barrier has been dealt with. She is aware of the difficulties that she has working with men or eating in public and has developed effective coping strategies to deal with these situations. Until Frances is confronted with the need to change, or she decides that she no longer wants to live with these problems she will continue to hide them and 'pretend' they are not there.

Learning points

- Change can expose underlying mental health problems.
- Clients can be adept at hiding psychological issues.
- Unexpected disclosures can lead to difficult situations.
- Question sensitively once a problem is noticed.
- Clients may try to use coaching as a way to maintain secrecy.
- Some people may be keen to maintain contact beyond the coaching, be cautious.

11

A stable life for Ghulam?

Issues of sexuality, bipolar affective disorder and narcissistic personality disorder are explored through the story of Ghulam, a second-generation immigrant from an Asian family who has been newly appointed to the role of sales director.

All company directors have coaching for the first six months in new positions. The coaching is face to face on company premises and is provided by a specialist executive coaching organisation. The coach is appointed, rather than chosen by the client.

During the first session the coach meets an articulate, intelligent man who is confident in his abilities and knows where he is going. His route to this appointment has been through several, fairly short, sales roles, each giving more responsibility and greater rewards. The coach thinks that Ghulam was an ideal recruit for the role. He fits the stereotype of a sales executive with his manner, motivation and attitude to work.

The first of the following three scenarios follows on from this with the coach feeling very happy with the coaching. Ghulam is positive, seems able to look at his actions and to adjust his work through the insights he gets in the sessions. He completes all tasks and is actively participating in the coaching. The coaching contract involves a short, written feedback report part way through.

Some days after this the coach gets an unexpected telephone call from the human resources director who says that she is somewhat surprised by the positive nature of the feedback as there have been problems with Ghulam and his inappropriate behaviour with subordinates. The coach learns that there have been complaints about Ghulam, that he is a bully, is rude and always finds someone to blame for any issue. The coach is left with the expectation that this problem will be addressed.

At the start of the next session the coach asks if Ghulam received his copy of the feedback report and if he has any comments.

Ghulam: 'I thought it was a true reflection of how the coaching is going and I'm very impressed that you have identified my abilities so professionally; you're really helping me settle in here.'

Coach: 'That wasn't the view of the human resources director.'

Ghulam: 'I wouldn't listen to her, she really doesn't like me. Between you and me she is incompetent and probably on the way out.'

Coach: 'OK, but I think we still need to look at these issues.'

Ghulam: 'We're facing some really difficult times and I'm pushing people at the moment. I'm still sorting out the mess my predecessor left behind and there are a couple of people who need sorting out too. That's all that's been going on.'

> [Superficially a plausible response, but the coach has had potential issues raised and will be more aware of anything further that may add to these early suspicions. Some information is stored in the corner.]

In a later session there has been some discussion of Ghulam using a coaching style of leadership with some of his team. He has mentioned going on a coaching course some time ago and it seems a sensible course of action to help him with some goals around pressure of work and delegating.

The session starts with the coach asking for feedback on these goals of delegating.

Ghulam: 'They can't do it, I've got to watch them the whole time, the other day Jim suggested that I'd got something wrong, how ridiculous is that!'

Coach: 'What makes you say that?'

Ghulam then starts a tirade against everyone he works with, how useless they are, how they can't do anything on their own. He had been denied an office refurbishment, his secretary had resigned, and good riddance, she was lazy.

The coach is quite shocked by the strength of his outburst, which seems so at odds with the usual Ghulam. The highlights are that it is never any of Ghulam's fault and that he is not receiving the recognition he deserves. The session ends with a comment from the coach about how angry Ghulam seems and a gentle reminder about the goal of improving delegation.

A few days later the coach finds out that Ghulam has made a complaint against the coach for inappropriate behaviour. This is very worrying for the coach and the coaching provider. This company is an important client, and the coaching company has a well-deserved reputation for professionalism to protect.

A week later the coaching provider is informed that Ghulam has left by mutual agreement and that the complaint has been withdrawn.

The key point in this scenario is the change in how Ghulam responded to the coaching. Whilst the coach was in a position to help, Ghulam was charming, flattering and gave every appearance of being the ideal client. Once some doubts had been raised with the views of the human resources director on the interim report and the coach started to be more sceptical, Ghulam switched from being friendly to attacking. Simplistically this is 'if you can't help me, then you're my enemy' and is a pointer to what may have been going on.

Someone behaving in this type of erratic and changeable way most likely has a personality disorder (see Chapter 17). In this case the suggestion is that this is a narcissistic personality, one of the antisocial personality disorders. Although coaching appeared to be progressing well at the beginning this was a pretence to keep the coach on side whilst this was useful. Once it was no longer possible to continue with the pretence the coach then became an enemy and was attacked.

Coaching will never be of benefit to someone with a personality disorder such as this. Any coach finding themselves in a situation like this would be best advised to be cautious, protect themselves and extricate themselves as soon as possible. This type of client can be very vindictive.

One issue that needs considering is how to inform others that coaching has stopped. In a situation such as this of business coaching there will need to be some explanation to the client company as to why coaching has ended prematurely. This may need more thought than a simple admission that coaching was not going to work in this case as there may be implications due to the specific contract. Detailed thought and discussion with a supervisor or other colleague, following the guidelines set out in Chapters 3 and 4, will give the best chance of an appropriate ending.

A problem of identity

In this scenario the coaching has a similar beginning, with the coach meeting an articulate and seemingly able 'ideal choice' for sales director.

The mid-point written feedback is well received by all, and the coach learns that Ghulam has become highly regarded. Ghulam reports that the coaching has been very helpful and a major factor in his early achievements.

The coach is shocked to hear from Ghulam that he is thinking of leaving.

Ghulam: 'This place isn't right for me.'
Coach: 'That's come as a real surprise, has something happened?
Ghulam: 'No, not really, it just isn't right.'
Coach: 'You seemed to be getting on really well, I've heard nothing but fantastic reports.'
          [At this point the coach may well be thinking that something has happened that has panicked Ghulam, possibly something personal.

Maybe he thinks he has made an error and
will be caught out or exposed.]

Ghulam: 'I know, this is a great place to work, but it isn't
right for me. Best to move on before anyone knows.'

[There is a clue here at the end, 'before
anyone knows'. The coach may start thinking about illegalities, malpractice or misconduct. The coach has respect for Ghulam,
the work has been going very well, and
probably cannot imagine he could have done
anything so bad that it cannot be solved.]

Coach: 'It can't be that bad, why don't we talk about it?

Ghulam: 'Sorry, but it's personal.'

Coach: [Silence, thinking of what to do.]

Ghulam: 'Look, I have feelings for other men, they're
wrong.'

Coach: 'Are you saying you're gay?'

Ghulam: [Silence.]

Coach: 'That doesn't matter, I wondered if you were gay,
it's completely OK here. The head of operations is
completely open about being gay, he brings his
partner to the company dinner.'

Ghulam: 'I can't be gay, it's against my faith, I'll go to hell.'

Many coaches will find themselves in situations where the
client shares very personal and intimate details. In this
scenario the coaching has been very successful and the
coach is genuinely surprised and puzzled when told that
the client is leaving the company and wants to see if this can
be avoided by offering to talk it over.

The story that unfolds is one of a very real point of
friction in the client's life. This is the dichotomy between
the importance of his faith and his feelings for other men. It
may be that this is a repeating pattern. Ghulam runs away
whenever he feels his feelings may be exposed.

Although to the coach and to the company Ghulam's
sexuality has little, if any, relevance, it is a point of enormous
anxiety to him. Anyone finding themselves in a situation
where core beliefs are at odds with feelings or circumstances
is likely to experience considerable psychological turbu-

lence. Someone may refuse to consider the idea of divorce, even if in an abusive or violent relationship, because marriage means 'until death do us part'. Psychological problems, which may lead to serious mental illness, can occur around mismatches of cultural norms and the circumstances the client finds themselves in. A female manager who has been brought up in a dominant male culture may have problems if promoted to team leader with the expectation of supervising men. Similarly, a male worker may struggle with a female manager if his culture of origin has been one of women 'knowing their place', or one where women are 'the weaker sex' and must be protected.

In this scenario, Ghulam has two main choices: to leave and repeat a cycle of running away when the issue of his sexuality arises or to try to find a resolution to his dilemma.

Neither of these are an issue that coaching can address. The coaching will end if he chooses to resign and he would be best advised to look for specialist support if he decided to try to find a resolution. It may take some time for anyone in this type of situation to find the best person or group to offer support – this could be a suitable counsellor, a self-help group, a faith-based group or other. A search on the internet could lead to some useful contact details; someone somewhere will have struggled through whatever the issue is that is leading to these types of problems.

If coaching were to continue, a useful adjunct to the main focus would be to support the client at work whilst the client finds their own way to resolve the issue. There is no case to break confidentiality, no reason to say anything to others, any disclosure needs to be the client's choice and in the client's time. Telling others because the coach thought this would help to ease any tensions would be in breach of any code of conduct. This could put pressure on the coach and the client as they have to hold these difficult secrets during coaching sessions.

From the organisation's perspective, as part of a three-way contract, the coaching has been a great success; Ghulam received great benefit until the point of deciding to leave. The organisation has no need to be told anything about the actual circumstances revealed in the session, during coaching, at the end or in the future. The coach would need to take care not to inadvertently disclose this privileged information at a later date.

A frightening direction

In this scenario coaching starts with the intelligent and articulate successful new sales director. The coach notes that Ghulam could almost be the stereotype for the job, from his fashionable and elegant dress and grooming to his motivations and positive outlook.

The coaching starts quite positively for a number of sessions. The coach starts to become envious, in a way, of this person who seems to have everything and to be able to do everything. Ghulam reports working very long hours, but also managing to play a lot of sports and socialising. The coach wondered where he got his money from as he talked of a new car, a second home on the coast and expensive gifts for several different women. Whilst listening to these sorts of stories was not really part of the coaching, they came out around his boasting about just how much he was going to achieve for the organisation. However extravagant that Ghulam's goals appeared, they were believable. With his power, energy and belief in himself anything seemed possible.

Ghulam bounces into the room for the next session, shaking the coach vigorously by the hand and launches into a long conversation with no clear meaning. His appearance has changed; he is quite dishevelled and looks like he hasn't had enough sleep.

Coach: 'Ghulam, Ghulam, slow down, can we start again please?'
Ghulam: 'Why, didn't you understand it, it's such a good idea, I can't wait to let everyone know.'
Coach: 'What idea?'
Ghulam: 'What I just said, . . .'
          [Ghulam restates with complete conviction that he intends to radically change the sales process in a way that the coach, with limited

sales experience, can see is completely unsound.]

Ghulam: '. . . this will increase turnover and double profits in three months.'

[Ghulam is pacing around, gesticulating, speaking very rapidly in a loud voice.]

[Something has changed for Ghulam and the coach should have warning bells ringing by now, but what is happening? A thought may be that he has been drinking, or that he has been using drugs. The coach recognises that this session is not going anywhere at the moment and tries to bring it back to something useful.]

Coach: 'Ghulam, calm down, come and sit down and let's start again.'

Ghulam: 'What the heck do you know, I'm the king, I'm the future.'

[The coach is confused and worried and decides to challenge Ghulam on what may be the most simplistic reason for his extreme behaviour – drinking.]

Coach: 'Have you been drinking?'

[An attempt to offer a rational explanation for this extreme behaviour.]

Ghulam: 'What do you mean, I don't drink, I follow Islam, you know that.'

[Challenging Ghulam is making him even more irritable.]

Coach: 'What is the matter then?'

Ghulam: [Leaning over the coach threateningly.] 'Nothing's the matter, you're stupid, that's the matter.'

[Do not respond in a challenging, combative or threatening way, this could precipitate violence.]

This is clearly seriously abnormal behaviour by now and Ghulam has become more agitated and quite threatening. Best practice under these circumstances is to end the session, not by asking, or demanding that Ghulam leave, but by walking out. Ghulam may choose to leave. Do not obstruct this, do not be tempted to try to restrain him in any way. This may result in violence.

The intention with this scenario is to try to paint a realistic picture of an extreme change in someone's behaviour. What has happened with Ghulam is consistent with an episode of mania, the manic phase of bipolar affective disorder as described in Chapter 17. There could be other final diagnoses and other causes of such an extreme episode. Dealing with any of these would be similar to dealing with bipolar affective disorder.

Whatever the setting, at work, in a consulting suite, a home office or meeting room, the first and primary action should be to ensure the safety of the coach and anyone else around. No good will be served and the client will not benefit if the coach takes risks and is physically harmed. Whenever possible take reasonable care for the person's immediate safety. The aim is to try to limit any damage they may do to themselves.

The priorities are to get immediate help for the coach and client. For the coach, get someone else involved for safety, if alone then call the police. For the client, care for their immediate safety, which means getting professional medical help immediately.

The choice may be to take Ghulam to his doctor or to an emergency treatment centre, probably best if there is a driver and a companion with Ghulam, just in case. If Ghulam became very agitated, perhaps aggressive or violent then call for emergency medical treatment, call the ambulance. Call an ambulance if there is no suitable alternative. Paramedics will have had training in how best to treat someone who is having a psychotic episode. Call the police if necessary, particularly if the client has become violent or is threatening violence. The route to help that is taken, ultimately, depends on individual circumstances and what would be the usual course of action locally.

The key message if you are ever faced with someone exhibiting severe agitation, psychosis, mania or other threatening behaviour is not to take any risks.

Once the immediate incident has been dealt with the

appropriate person needs to inform the next of kin of the episode. This may be the coach or the human resources department in an organisation for example. In a business setting there is a responsibility to the rest of the staff and the person needs to be signed off sick and, maybe, denied access to the workplace. Trying to play down the severity of the problem by taking a 'he will be OK tomorrow' attitude will be risky.

It is possible that a response and apology may follow an episode such as this. If there is a suggestion, or presumption, that coaching will continue, the appropriate advice is to say no. Trust will have gone. Could the coach continue working with the client after being threatened? Almost certainly not. As with most cases where the coach takes action beyond the contract and outside the professional coaching relationship, there is no going back to 'normal'.

Conclusions

The title of this chapter suggests that Ghulam is looking for a stable life. In the first scenario, which suggests an anti-social personality disorder or narcissistic personality, the stability is driven by the client's need to always be right, no matter what the evidence is to suggest otherwise. The values and belief system that this type of person is living revolve around themselves, their perfection and their right to have what they want. This type of person will use any means to defend this position – lying, cheating and doing others down for example. They are unlikely to allow any credence to another's view and will be adept at the excuse; any issues will always be someone else's fault, no matter how strong the evidence. The primary goal of any coach faced with someone like this is to look after themselves and extricate themselves from the situation in a professional manner.

The stable life that Ghulam is looking for in the second scenario is for some way to balance the conflicting drives of his religion and cultural upbringing with an incompatible belief, his homosexuality. He will not find stability and a way to be comfortable with himself until this is resolved. This type of conflict is probably more common than is generally thought and can lead to a wide range of mental health problems. Not all will be as clear cut as the examples given above. Anyone whose ethical and moral values are at odds with what they are doing or being asked to do could end up suffering psychological problems. In medicine this could be making choices on treatment based on financial priorities. In law it could be having to defend the indefensible. In commerce someone may struggle to take financially prudent decisions when this will harm others, with redundancy for example. As with so many areas of potential mental health problems the list of issues is endless, the way forward when they arise is usually quite similar.

For someone who has such severe problems as Ghulam in the final scenario, stability is only likely to be found with the help provided by the medical profession and drug treatment long term.

Learning points

- The unknown can end coaching.
- The client's values and beliefs matter, not those generally held in society.
- There will be occasions when the coach must protect themselves.
- Anyone severely agitated needs careful treatment.
- Sometimes nothing more can be done.

12

Who is Hilary?

The coach meets a very unusual person in Hilary and struggles to make sense of what is going on.

There is a telephone message first thing one morning from an excited-sounding woman who introduces herself as Hilary and says she has seen the coach's website and 'it is just what I need'. Unfortunately no telephone number has been left so the coach cannot return the call.

A couple of days later the coach receives an e-mail message from Hilary via the website. The coach responds pointing out that no telephone number was given in the message. They agree a time to talk.

At the appointed time the session starts and lasts for 40 minutes. After the call is over the coach thinks back over the session, looking at the notes taken. It is a confusing picture with no coherent story or clear picture of what Hilary wants to achieve. Hilary has mentioned:

- Two teenage children and how demanding they are.
- A husband somewhere in the past, but the coach is unclear if they are divorced or separated, when the relationship broke down and how much contact they now have.
- Some form of clerical job, that seems to leave quite a lot of free time but was also described as important and full of responsibility with colleagues calling on Hilary at any time for help.
- A vague list of desires for the future that seemed to include every possible aspect of her life: children, home, a

perfect partner, fulfilling career, health, fitness and body image.

The coach was puzzled as to how the usual plan of a first session had been completely lost. She hadn't managed to talk about how coaching would work, expectations of results, practicalities of missing or changing sessions and contact between sessions as would normally be expected. In the last ten minutes the coach tried to impose some focus, trying to become clear what it was that Hilary hoped to achieve from the coaching. Hilary agreed to e-mail a list of three things she wanted to achieve in the next three months and explain how achieving them would improve her life.

Two days before the next session a clear and detailed e-mail arrives from Hilary, stating three tasks and how achieving them would enhance her life. The tasks are:

1 To change her work practices so that work does not have such an impact on home life.
2 To rebuild a good relationship with her children and help them grow up effectively, as Hilary is concerned she has been neglecting them and wants to enjoy their company before it is too late.
3 To find time for herself, to make new friends, have some fun and enjoy her life before she is too old. Hilary says she has been too preoccupied recently and has forgotten how to have fun.

At the beginning of the next session the coach starts by going over the practicalities of the coaching that were missed during the first session.

Hilary: 'That all sounds fine.'
Coach: 'I just need to be clear about the practicalities of the coaching . . .'
Hilary: [Interrupting] '. . . I know, I know and I appreciate that, but all this is on the website isn't it?'
Coach: 'Yes it is, but I just need to be sure that our contract is clear.'
Hilary: 'Contract! Good grief it sounds like I'm buying a business! Hang on I'm writing an e-mail to say I've

        read all the small print and I agree to it all, how's that?'

Coach: 'Thank you.'

        [The coach cannot think of anything else to say. Hilary appears to be a very different type of client to what the coach has previously experienced.]

Hilary: 'There you go, that's written and sent, now, I've gone on a diet, lost four pounds already, I've let myself go recently and that's not good, I went swimming the other morning and could only manage 12 lengths before I had to get out absolutely exhausted and Susie and I are going for a big shop, my wardrobe is so out of date . . .'

Coach: 'Who's Susie?'

Hilary: 'My daughter, Marcus mind you, he's grounded, he bought some stuff on E-bay without permission to impress his friends, no harm done, but I'm not having that, it's so hard to have to deal with all that sort of stuff without a man around, don't you think?'

Coach: 'Well, yes, it sounds it. Shall we look at your goals and what you want to achieve?'

Hilary: 'You're so clever, how did you know that I needed to achieve three things? It was brilliant to work them out and then write them down, now I've told you I'll have to do them won't I?' [Laughing.]

Coach: 'Quite a lot of people say that writing things down is a good aid to actually making them happen. Shall we start by looking at the first one?'

        [As with the first session, the coach is finding it difficult to feel involved in the conversation. Hilary seems to want to talk and talk.]

Hilary: 'What was that?'

        [The coach had been pleased to receive a detailed and obviously well-thought-out list of objectives prior to the session but now Hilary does not appear to be able to remember the first one.]

Coach: 'You said you wanted to make changes at work so that it does not have such an impact on home life.'

Hilary: 'Oh that one. I've sorted that, I had a meeting with the MD and things will change over the next few months. It went really well, we both agree it's for the best. It was quite a relief really and so easy when we sat down and talked.'

[It is only two days since Hilary e-mailed the coach with this topic as her first priority.]

Coach: 'Oh! Wonderful, how will your work change?'

Hilary: 'Bob is going to take early retirement, it's a pity, he's such a sweetie, but he agrees he can't handle the job anymore. Marcus really needs my attention, but I'm not sure how to go about that. We don't share any interests, not like Susie, we can do girlie things together and that's fun.'

Coach: 'Hilary, a moment please, I'm getting confused.'

Hilary: 'Oh sorry, everyone says I talk too much and too fast. I think that Marcus taking my credit card was a cry for attention, but spending time with him is much harder than with Susie, what do you think I should do? I can't stand his music tastes, I hate computer games, I watch him play football sometimes but that's not doing anything together is it? We could go skiing I suppose, but Susie would be a problem, she takes all my attention, she's so much slower than us, Marcus won't like that, he'll get bored and whiz off on his own, that would defeat the object wouldn't it?'

What is going on? The coach has been listening to Hilary now for some time without any real input. The conversation is jumping around from topic to topic, with lots of loose ends and no focus or apparent purpose. But, Hilary seems happy to talk and excited about changing her life. She appears in total control of the session.

A short time later, after Hilary has decided a skiing holiday with Marcus is a good idea, and that Susie will be bribed by plenty of shopping to stay at home, the session comes to a surprising end.

Hilary: 'Well that's our 40 minutes up, I've really enjoyed myself today, you've been so helpful, thank you very much, see you in two weeks.'

Coach: 'Yes, two weeks, thank you. But what about . . .'

Hilary: 'Bye then.'

This has been a bizarre session; the coach is left exhausted and confused and takes time to reflect on what happened.

- Similarly to the first session, Hilary has seemed bored and irritated with the practicalities of coaching, but she sent an e-mail immediately to acknowledge her understanding of the contractual obligations.
- Hilary talks and talks, flitting about from one topic to the next.
- She talks of people as though the coach must know them, Bob, Marcus, the coach is left guessing who they are. The coach managed to get clarification that Susie is Hilary's daughter.
- She asks questions, then doesn't give time for an answer or answers them herself.
- She seems highly excitable, with pressured speech (rapid, staccato speech with little or confused meaning).
- Some sense of grandiosity; who could solve a major work–home life problem within two days, and by the MD retiring? Just go skiing as a way to be close to her son?
- There is a sense that if Hilary says it will happen it will, with a certain unbelievable quality, a lack of reality, maybe even delusions.
- The ending: Hilary must have been keeping an eye on the time to bring the session to an ending in this way, she gave thanks to the coach, said the session had been helpful and confirmed the next contact without allowing the coach to respond.

From the first telephone call, when no return number was left, through the first and, finally, the second session Hilary has shown many signs of unusual behaviour. Some of these would suggest a possible mental health issue. There are signs that would suggest a personality disorder (see Chapter 17), broadly classified as 'an extreme deviation from the way an average person in a particular culture perceives, thinks, feels and relates to others' (ICD-10 definition) but Hilary does not match any particular personality type. There are elements that could indicate the restlessness and inattention of ADHD or even the behaviours, which may be the prodrome or pre-cursor to a psychotic episode. Some of these behaviours could be linked to use of drugs that may have affected her emotional stability.

Broadly speaking she seems to live in a world of her own, talking at the coach rather than holding a conversation and unable to maintain a train of thought for long before becoming more interested in the next thought.

The coach takes the opportunity to discuss Hilary with her supervisor; jointly they decide that there is nothing specific and no action to be taken at this stage, but that effort needs to be taken to try to manage the sessions more and to bring some coherency to Hilary's story and goals.

The coach decides to e-mail Hilary a few days before the next planned session asking for an idea on what she would like to focus on. The earlier e-mail had produced a positive response; asking for goals had seemed to catalyse Hilary into action, maybe another would be beneficial?

Hilary replies:

> Thank goodness you mailed me, I'd totally forgotten in my excitement. I'll have to cancel the next one, of course I'll pay – that's what the terms and conditions say isn't it – see I did read them :~)).
>
> Marcus and I are going to the mountains for a few days, it's really exciting, can I phone you on the 25th, I think that's our next session isn't it?
> Love
> Hilary
> PS: I've bought the sexiest new ski outfit, it's bright pink!!!!

An unusual communication to receive to cancel a coaching session, but it does cover all necessary points. Another layer to the story of Hilary's coaching, if it can be called that, as little if any coaching has taken place so far.

The coach waits for the next session with some nervousness, not knowing what to expect. The telephone rings and the coach picks up the call, exactly on time.

Hilary: 'Hi, how are? I've got so much to tell you, I was desperate to call you early but I'm not allowed to am I? The skiing trip was brilliant Marcus and I talked and talked and had such a laugh . . .'

    [Hilary goes straight into her monologue as before and the coach feels de-skilled and confused. What is going on?]

Hilary: '. . .and the skiing has had another bonus, I'm swimming about 20 lengths now most mornings without getting out of breath.'

    [This sounds like it is developing into a repeat of the last session. The coach decides to intervene and try to bring some coaching focus into the conversation.]

Coach: 'That all sounds wonderful, Hilary. I wonder if we might just focus on the coaching for a moment?'

    [A gentle intervention first.]

Hilary: 'Oh, I thought I was.'

    [It sounds like Hilary thought she was engaged in the activity of coaching all along. A statement that the coach doesn't think coaching is taking place is too harsh. Hilary's view that she has been being coached gives the pointer to an approach that the coach follows.]

Coach: 'I see, what were you expecting from coaching?'

Hilary: 'Just this, you listen while I talk about my problems and I have to work out my own solutions. Isn't that right? That's what your website says.'

    [Which could be an interpretation of a description of coaching, if somewhat limited and naive.]

Coach: 'Well, that's part of it certainly, but there is normally more. I'm struggling to see what help I am being at the moment . . .'

Hilary: [Interrupting] 'Oh, you're being a great help, I feel so positive and life is so much more fun now.'

Coach: 'And I'm really pleased for you. Part of my job is to help you understand what you have changed and how so that you can learn how to use these skills again in the future.'

Hilary: 'What do you mean?'

Coach: 'Well, for example, you wanted to change how you worked. Last time we spoke you said that that was sorted and the MD was going to retire. I'm struggling to see how that would help you.'

Hilary: 'Oh! That's easy, Bob is 62, he only stayed on to help me after Mum died and if we find a good managing director I won't have to be as involved in the company.'

Coach: 'What is your place in the company?'

Hilary: 'It's mine, well nearly all of it, it's a family business. Mum loved being involved, but I don't, I struggle.'

The missing pieces start to fall into place.

The underlying story doesn't really matter as part of this description of a possible mental health issue, but, for completion: Hilary is divorced with two children, her mother died two years ago. Hilary took over her mother's place in the family business, which she struggled with. This distracted her from her children and left little space for a personal life. Hilary has been used to long rambling telephone calls with her mother, the only person she has turned to for help in the past, and takes a similar approach with the coach because this always worked in the past.

As detailed above, there are several signs that may suggest some mental health issue, but, signs of mental illness form a part of normal behaviour, and in this case focusing on them or giving them undue credence would have been an error.

The dialogue may sound far-fetched, would anyone contact a coach and then behave as Hilary has? One of the authors (AB) has met at least two clients who behaved in broadly similar ways in the last ten years.

There are those clients who:

- Have their own interpretation on what will happen.
- Have their own view on the relationship and the boundaries.

- Talk with the expectation that the coach understands everything without explanation.
- Show little interest in exploring issues.
- Decide on a course of action and then just do it.
- Report unbelievably quick progress on meeting goals.

Whilst clients who behave in these ways can be confusing at first, they are not showing signs of mental illness. Psychological issues and mental health problems are only one explanation of what may be going on when an unusual client appears. The unexpected and unexplainable are as likely to be due to an idiosyncratic personality as mental illness.

In this scenario, Hilary has shown signs that could be interpreted as psychological problems, such as the care she gives to get things right, her lack of attention, her disorganised way of communicating and her apparent lack of thought for others when choosing a course of action. These are issues that could, theoretically, be helped by therapy but Hilary lives a fruitful life. She has shown in this short dialogue an ability to build relationships and care for others and is generally successful and happy.

Should the coach find a client with similarities to Hilary the decision on the way forward is best viewed as a personal one – does the coach feel comfortable continuing? Little if any coaching in its formal sense will happen, but Hilary says she is benefiting from the relationship, she is making changes that help meet her stated goals.

With credit to Dr Spock and Captain Kirk of Star Trek fame: 'It's coaching, Jim, but not as we know it.'

Conclusions

The story of Hilary has been included at the end of this section, 'What's being said?', as a counterpoint to the exploration of mental illness in the previous chapters. When meeting anyone who shows unusual behaviour it is of equal importance to discount mental illness as to prove it. The critical point is to discount the behaviour rather than ignore it. Any unusual behaviour, anything that a client says that is bizarre, not based in reality or incongruent with what would normally be expected needs attention.

Changes in client behaviour are the expectation of successful coaching, managing and mentoring. Occasionally, changes will indicate something other than the client's positive personal development. Be ready to take appropriate action when these occur.

Learning points

- Signs of mental illness are all around.
- They can be found, if looked for, in many conversations.
- A balanced approach is needed before deciding if action needs be taken.
- View the client holistically, before forming a view.
- Explore what is being said from the client's viewpoint before making a judgement.
- The unusual, even the bizarre, may have a rational explanation.
- An idiosyncratic personality is not mental illness.

But
- Mental illness kills.
- If undetected and untreated, years of hardship can follow.
- Signs can be subtle and difficult to identify.
- When in doubt:
    - ➤ be cautious; seek expert advice
    - ➤ be cautious; do not add to the client's difficulties
    - ➤ be cautious; avoid future problems and blame.

SECTION 3

Categories of mental illness, their definition, epidemiology and management

This section will provide a brief overview of the more common mental illnesses as defined medically; these are grouped in clusters of similar issues.

The aim is not to provide the facility for coaches and other related professionals to provide a diagnosis but to offer a different route to learning. By using this section, the reader will gain insight into the variety of mental illnesses and their likely prognosis. When a coach meets someone with signs of mental illness the most likely outcome is that coaching will stop and the coach is unlikely to find out how the client has got on. The 'wondering' that the coach may experience can be helped by some knowledge of what is likely to happen to their client in the future.

What follows is a brief guide to what the diagnostic words mean, and a suggestion of available treatments. For more detailed descriptions, a standard psychiatry text such as the *New Oxford Book of Psychiatry* (Gelder et al., 2003) will give access to current thinking. Throughout this section there are numerous statistics offered to aid the reader in gaining an understanding of the issues. These are not individually referenced and are offered as a guide only. A more precise knowledge of the prevalence and prognosis of mental health issues will be found in an academic psychiatry publication as suggested above.

The diagnosis and management of mental health problems are not easy. There are numerous textbooks for specialists that berate experienced general and family doctors for failing to diagnose a mental health problem. Yet these same doctors rarely miss significant physical illnesses. So there must be something different about mental health problems.

Equally, in the early stages of illness psychiatrists will often be unsure about the eventual diagnosis and best treatment. The old joke 'how many psychiatrists does it take to change a light bulb?' answer: 'only one but the light bulb has really got to want to change', also well illustrates the need for the patient to accept that there is a problem and cooperate with the treatment recommended.

Probably only HIV and AIDS carry as much stigma as a mental illness in the minds of the general public.

Is it any wonder it is often masked and denied by the sufferer?

13

Depressive illnesses

This chapter looks at a variety of mental illnesses where the person is showing signs of depression. These are the changes in mood and behaviours that range from normal unhappiness to persistent depressive thoughts, feelings and actions and may result in deliberate self-harm, suicidal thoughts and attempted suicide. It is likely to be the most common mental health problem encountered by the coach or other in a professional relationship.

Grief and bereavement

This is a normal human condition and would not usually be described as a mental illness, but as the signs and symptoms of grieving are similar to depression it has been included in this chapter for clarity.

We all lose those we love and suffer as a consequence. There are 'stages' of grief that we all go through and these are described as follows:

1 First, an initial numbness when there is a feeling of unreality, the fact of the death is not fully accepted.
2 This is followed by a period of sadness with weeping, loss of sleep and appetite, and very much mimics a depressive illness. The person will often express guilt that 'more could have been done' and may be angry with themselves or those around them.
3 Then, finally, comes a period of resolution and acceptance.

The expression of grief is strongly linked to culture and belief, and people should be allowed to grieve in their own way.

Most people simply need compassion, reassurance and the chance to talk about the one they have lost. The listener may well not be able to say or do anything 'to make things better', but good listening is indeed the key to helping recovery. There are excellent services available in the voluntary sector and most general practice surgeries and primary care physicians will have access to counselling as necessary. Only rarely are drugs indicated, although a short course of anxiolytics or sleeping tablets may be offered in the early stages.

If the grief becomes prolonged, generally regarded as affecting functioning beyond six months, the client may be described as suffering from an abnormal grief reaction and may need more intense intervention with antidepressant tablets, psychotherapy or referral to a psychiatrist. This occurs in those people particularly vulnerable to the loss or who are prevented from expressing their grief in the normal way. A past history of depression may also be a predisposing factor in prolonging grief. Rarely does the bereaved person express suicidal ideas, general feelings of worthlessness or have severe motor retardation (a slowing of movement). These would ring alarm bells and need prompt action and referral to the appropriate medical practitioner.

In general, once the client has passed the severe distress of early bereavement it should be possible to continue coaching although working with a truly depressed client is of little value as their muddled and slow thinking and feelings of worthlessness will preclude any useful change.

It is worth noting that grieving can follow on from a wide variety of losses, not just the death of a loved one. The loss and potential loss of anything important can lead to grieving, which may be painful and follow a similar course to the death of a loved one as described above.

For example, the break-up of a relationship may lead to grieving. In Chapter 5, Andrea's story, she could well have been behaving in a superficially similar way if she had split up with her boyfriend.

Similarly, the loss of an expectation can lead to grieving, for example a woman discovers that she cannot conceive or a person is forced to give up an important sporting activity due to illness or injury. The list is endless, but the prognosis is similar. When any of us lose something important to our lives we need to adjust to a new way of living without it. During the period of adjustment the benefit of coaching may be reduced and it may be more appropriate to suggest other ways of getting help.

Depression

Many people feel they know what depression is yet there is no general agreement about the best method of classifying a depressive illness. There are currently two main systems used. ICD-10 (International Classification of Diseases – Tenth Revision, WHO 1994) and DSM-IV (Diagnostic and Statistical Manual of Mental Disorder – Fourth Edition, American Psychiatric Association 1994). However for practical and clinical purposes it is often most useful to use a descriptive approach and leave the formal classifications for research purposes.

Descriptively, depression is a lowering of mood and a loss of interest or pleasure in activities that are normally enjoyed. At any point in time 1 in 10 people will have a depressive illness and the lifetime risk of depression is 12 per cent for men and 25 per cent for women. At least 40 per cent of general practice consultations in the UK are for psychiatric problems and most of these will be depression (or anxiety and depression). Many of these may go unrecognised, particularly in those patients who present with somatic (physical) features of depression.

Rather like the 'normal' process of bereavement a depressed mood is a common and normal experience in everyone's life. What distinguish the mental health problems of a depressive illness are the severity, persistence and duration of the symptoms (see symptoms of depression listed below).

There is also a milder but persistent mood disorder usually described as Dysthymia, when some of the symptoms of depression are present but not in sufficient severity or number to be called a mental illness. Someone with this persistent mild depression could be described as a 'moaning Minnie', or as 'always miserable'. They would be euphemistically described as a 'cup half empty' person rather than a 'cup half full' person. Dysthymia may interfere with social or work achievements and could have an impact on coaching.

Seasonal Affective Disorder (SAD), although not universally recognised by the medical profession, may be classed as a type of depressive illness that comes and goes depending on the time of year. It is linked to available light levels, and, hence, coaches may find themselves with a client who has been active in the coaching sessions and then starts to show signs of depression as winter approaches. Should this occur then the client is best served by approaching them as if they were depressed, allowing the medical profession to decide if SAD is the cause of the low mood.

Symptoms of depression

- Prolonged markedly depressed mood
- Loss of interest or enjoyment in usual activities
- Feelings of guilt or worthlessness
- Reduced confidence
- Ideas of deliberate self-harm or suicide
- Disturbed sleep
- Disturbed appetite
- Diminished libido
- Feelings of fatigue
- Poor concentration.

Much has also been written about the definition or difference between depression and anxiety and except for research purposes is probably of little consequence. Most people with a depressive illness exhibit some features of anxiety and vice versa.

There are also a number of other medical conditions that can give a combination of the listed symptoms and at first presentation to a medical practitioner the patient will have a thorough physical check-up which may well involve blood tests. The types of diseases that may be discovered include Hypothyroidism (underactive thyroid gland), alcoholism and substance misuse (drug addiction).

There are several treatment options for depression and the decision on suitability depends to some extent on the severity of the disease and also on patient choice. In general, the basic decision is between 'talking' therapies and/or drug treatment.

Psychotherapy and counselling

The majority of depressed patients will benefit from psychotherapy or counselling either alone or in combination with drugs. In mild to moderate depression 'talking' therapies are as effective as tablets and are the first choice of many patients. They require trained and skilled individuals and are resource intensive. Access to them through the patient's doctor varies. They can be purchased privately but cost may be an issue.

Drug treatments

There are a number of different categories of drugs available in the management of depression, all with benefits and disadvantages. Treatment needs to be tailored to each individual and will depend on response, side effects and previous experience to psychotropic medication. Broadly, the drugs can be divided into the 'older' drugs such as tricyclic antidepressants and MAOIs (monoamine oxidase inhibitors) that are effective, but are often limited by their side effects (they also have many interactions with other drugs and are potentially lethal in overdose), or the 'newer' drugs such as the SSRIs (selective serotonin reuptake inhibitors) and their derivatives. These are better tolerated by many patients, have fewer interactions and are much safer in overdose. Unfortunately, there have been recent concerns about their safety, in particular with regard to their withdrawal and with an increased risk of agitation and the possibility of suicidal ideation.

ECT and severe depression

It is worth briefly mentioning ECT (electro convulsive therapy) and severe depression. Severe depression or 'psychotic'
depression is a very serious illness associated with hallucinations and delusions in addition to the symptoms outlined
above. Hallucinations are things seen, heard, smelt, sensed
or tasted that are not actually present and delusions are
a false belief held against all rational argument and outside the cultural norm (for example that your neighbour
is pumping gas into your house to kill you). This illness
will require combinations of drugs such as antidepressants
and antipsychotic tablets or may need ECT. Despite the
sensationalism given by films such as 'One Flew Over the
Cuckoo's Nest', ECT has saved many lives and will continue
to do so, although the need for it has declined with the
improvement in drug therapies.

The diagnosis and treatment of depression is not
straightforward but the prognosis is good and as such every
effort should be made to get appropriate help for an individual. If the coach suspects their client has a depressive
illness then every effort should be made to encourage them
to acknowledge the problem and seek help. In the first
instance the family doctor is the usual source of confirm-
ation of the diagnosis and advice. Some individuals may
seek help from counsellors or therapists in the private sector
but most clients should be encouraged to see their doctor
as well. This will be useful to exclude physical illness and
assess the severity of the depression and in particular any
suicide risk.

Suicidal thoughts, ideas and deliberate self-harm

Suicide, just the word can bring fear into the mind of many,
but the fact is that anyone who wants to take their own life
will succeed, if not at first attempt then later.

Unlike the previous discussions this is clearly not part
of the normal spectrum. Although many of us experience
transient feelings of hopelessness these do not translate into
suicide or attempted suicide in the majority of cases.

Most people who attempt suicide will have told someone beforehand and this may be the coach or other helping professional. Views shared may be along the lines of 'I wish I was dead', to 'there's no future' and 'I wish it would all end'. Someone with suicidal thoughts and ideas may also do things in a way that suggest a 'tidying up' of their life before it ends, such as giving things away or sorting out personal affairs, which, in the work context, may be preparing for someone else to take over or not doing tasks that won't be needed until they have gone. In some there is a calm serenity once the decision to end their life has been accepted. This can give a false impression of improvement, particularly in those who have demonstrated a depressive illness in the recent past.

What is clear is that talking about suicide with a client, even discussing method, does not increase the risk of the completed act. The relief felt by the individual in being able to express these thoughts and the recognition of the depths of their despair may enable the client to seek life-saving help and they should be actively encouraged to do so.

The coach needs to be aware that the client's preferred method of suicide is a clear indication of the level of risk. Someone who expresses thoughts about 'ending it all' but with no clear idea about how, has not progressed to the same level of risk as the client who clearly states that they are going to use a violent and irreversible method such as a firearm or jumping from a height. There is a lethality hierarchy that incorporates both the chosen method of suicide and the chances of discovery and successful intervention by a third party. Someone who takes an overdose at home when their spouse is expected back is less likely to be successful than the individual who drives to a remote spot, hides the car and then takes an overdose. Whilst the coach may explore some of these issues around suicide in the meeting, an assessment of risk is a skilled job and *all* must be referred to an appropriate professional. Not all people who kill themselves have a psychiatric illness, but in those who do, depression is the most common.

Much has also been written about the link between deliberate self-harm (DSH) and subsequent suicide. DSH is probably most commonly thought of as cutting oneself, but includes any action of harm that is intentional. In those who have an episode of DSH there is an increased risk of subsequent suicide, with about 1 in 100 dying through suicide within a year.

Any intimation of suicidal thoughts should be taken seriously and prompt urgent action. Similarly, if you become aware that one of your clients has been self-harming, take it seriously and take action.

Neither suicidal thoughts and ideas nor someone self-harming are cases where a coach can sensibly carry on. Take action without delay.

Suicide cannot always be prevented. If you have the misfortune to be working with someone who commits suicide, recognise the huge impact this will have on you and seek help and support, and recommend it for anyone else closely involved.

Increased risk factors for suicide

- Male
- Over 40 years
- Psychiatric illness
- Previous attempts
- Drug or alcohol misuse
- Chronic physical illness
- Recent adverse event, e.g. bereavement/divorce/redundancy
- Social isolation.

Summary

Depression ranges from the daily, normal, stress-reducing 'pushing to one side' of uncomfortable feelings through the low mood and associated behaviours of grieving a loss to a persistent group of signs and symptoms best termed 'depressive illness'. This may lead to suicidal thoughts and intentions.

Along this spectrum people will show signs of a whole range of symptoms:

- Low or sad mood
- Loss of interest or pleasure
- Disturbed sleep
- Poor concentration
- Disturbed appetite
- Suicidal thoughts or acts
- Guilt or low self-worth
- Loss of self-confidence
- Pessimism or hopelessness about the future
- Fatigue or loss of energy
- Agitation or slowing of movement or speech
- Decreased libido
- Diurnal mood variation.

Anxiety or nervousness is also often present.

14

Anxiety, phobia and stress

Stress and anxiety are day-to-day parts of every human experience, yet what one individual finds stressful may evoke no response in another. Levels of anxiety also vary markedly from one person to another and are often dependent on the context within which the anxiety occurs; phobias are a good example of this. It is important to remember that from the client's point of view these emotions are real and often unpleasant experiences.

Anxiety and panic disorder

Anxiety is a normal human emotion and appropriate levels of anxiety will enhance performance. For example moderate levels of anxiety before an exam or interview will increase alertness and functioning. Even high levels of anxiety have a place in situations of real danger, enabling a quick response that may be life saving. Severe anxiety on the other hand is unhelpful and can rob the client of the ability to perform to any acceptable level. An anxiety disorder is not merely feeling more anxious than the rest of the population; the person affected will have specific or recurring fears that they will recognise as irrational. It is an unpleasant situation characterised by fearfulness and multiple physical symptoms. In normal anxiety, attention is focused on the threatening situation, whilst in a pathological situation, attention will also be focused on physical symptoms such as a racing heart. These people will be multiple users of medical services, as they believe that their symptoms represent serious disease.

Management is always a balancing act between treating the symptoms seriously and not increasing the anxiety by over investigation. Getting a heart tracing done may be reassuring the first time but if the doctors keep doing it there must be something really wrong, or so the anxious mind will think. Mixed anxiety and depression is also common and indeed their coexistence is only of real relevance in research. It is important to exclude depression before treating pure anxiety but management of the two conditions is very similar.

Generalised anxiety disorder (GAD)

- Nervousness or restlessness
- Trembling
- Difficulty sleeping
- Sweating
- Poor concentration
- Palpitations
- Frequent urination
- Tiredness
- Irritability
- Dizziness
- Breathlessness
- Low mood.

About 5 per cent of the population will suffer from GAD with a slight female preponderance but it will account for up to 30 per cent of psychiatric consultations in primary care. It starts at any time of life but usually between 20 and 40 years of age. It is generally a chronic disorder, which develops gradually and may have periods of remission. Stress is highly likely to precipitate a relapse. Under this circumstance a coach may well find themselves presented with a client whose physical health may be an initial concern, particularly if they have chest pain or breathlessness. Recognition of GAD and precipitating stressors would be a major advance in improving the client's functioning and their ability to achieve appropriate goals.

The mainstay of treatment for GAD has been drugs.

Benzodiazepines have a fast onset of action and are extremely effective, but their use is severely limited by their ability to produce dependence quickly. There are still patients on long-term benzodiazepines who were treated for anxiety in the 1970s. These days they would be limited to a short course (3–4 weeks) of treatment in very severe anxiety. Antidepressant drugs such as the tricyclics and SSRIs have anxiolytic properties in addition to their antidepressant effects and do not cause dependence. They can be used in the long-term management of this chronic disease. There are also a group of drugs called beta blockers whose primary use is in heart disease and high blood pressure but which have useful effects in GAD. They slow the heart, reduce sweating and calm a tremor; by removing these physical symptoms the client may well cope much better. In addition they can be used on an 'as required' basis when the client is troubled by symptoms. They are very useful for things like driving-test nerves. Unfortunately, they do have some significant side effects and interactions but are worth exploring with the doctor for particular clients who may be struggling to function to their true ability because of anxiety.

Psychological treatments include simple reassurance, problem solving counselling, cognitive behaviour therapy and anxiety management. Therapies are aimed at teaching skills to recognise and manage the symptoms of anxiety. They are as effective as drugs, although local availability may be an issue. Rebreathing into a paper bag can rapidly terminate an acute episode of hyperventilation.

Cognitive behaviour therapy (CBT) has many uses and there is increasing evidence for its effectiveness. It aims to identify maladaptive behaviours that recur in life and teach the client to recognise and modify them. Relaxation therapy is also very useful and can be used as an adjunct in both drug treatment and psychological therapies.

Panic disorder

Panic attacks may occur as part of many conditions, but panic disorder involves recurrent and unpredictable attacks of panic. The attacks start suddenly with pronounced physical features (see below) and are not restricted to specific situations.

Features of panic attacks

- Breathlessness
- Hyperventilation
- Dry mouth
- Faintness
- Chest pain
- Racing heart
- Sweating
- 'Butterflies' in the stomach
- Feeling of impending doom.

About 20 per cent of the population will experience at least one panic attack but only 2 per cent will have the severe disorder. It occurs most commonly between adolescence and the mid-thirties; it is very unusual for it to start after the age of 45. Its course is variable, sometimes episodic and varying in severity over time. There does appear to be a genetic predisposition.

Treatment options include the benzodiazepines or antidepressants. Psychological therapies that are effective include CBT, psychotherapy and relaxation therapy. In this condition a combination of psychological therapy after introducing drug therapy to control symptoms seems most effective.

Obsessive-compulsive disorder (OCD)

Once believed to be rare and immortalised in the film 'As good as it gets' with Jack Nicholson, this condition appears to be more common than was previously thought. It affects men and women equally and occurs in about 2 per cent of the population. It presents with repetitive and irrational thoughts that intrude on all aspects of life. The client has to gain peace of mind by carrying out behaviours to nullify the risk. These are often ritualistic and the client will experience severe anxiety that is temporarily relieved by completing the ritual. Examples of this are checking locks repeatedly or washing hands extensively. The thought 'my hands are dirty' will trigger a hand-washing ritual, but unfortunately the relief of anxiety felt by completing the ritual is only short lived. In addition, unless the ritual is performed perfectly it may have to be repeated again and again. There may also be avoidance behaviour, which could present in the workforce because an individual will not do photocopying, for example, in case they get ink on their hands. The symptoms of OCD are controlling, frustrating and irritating for both the individual and those around them. At least a third of people affected will have a chronic disorder with a fluctuating course. The outlook is worse if the personality is obsessive, the symptoms are severe and circumstances are stressful. Treatment needs to be by a specialist and is aimed at behavioural therapies that enable the person to gain control of their disorder and not respond to triggers with rituals. The newer antidepressants such as the SSRIs have shown some benefit.

Phobias

The symptoms of phobic anxiety disorder are the same as for GAD (see above) but occur in specific situations. There are two additional features that are seen: avoidance of the situation that provokes anxiety and anticipatory anxiety when there is the possibility of being in that situation. A phobia develops after an anxious person first experiences anxiety in a specific situation and then starts to avoid the situation and leaves quickly if confronted with it. There is then a vicious circle when the avoidance of the situation reduces anxiety and gives a positive gratifying feeling, reinforcing the phobia further. In general, the classification of these disorders is divided into specific or simple phobias, agoraphobia and social phobia; many simple phobias cause little impairment in functioning for the client and may well never become an issue that needs resolving but more severe phobia is a seriously disabling condition.

Simple or specific phobias

Symptoms

- Extreme, persistent and unreasonable fear
- Specific objects or situations trigger response, e.g. animals, heights, blood, flying, enclosed spaces, etc.
- The situation is avoided.

Management

- Behaviour therapy involving exposure, desensitisation, flooding and modelling
- Psychodynamic psychotherapy
- Drugs are of little use although a benzodiazepine may help in specific circumstances such as flying or as an adjunct in behaviour therapy.

These phobias are very common, affecting up to 10 per cent of the population but very few people seek help with them. They usually begin in childhood when phobias are common but why they persist in some people through to adulthood is not known. Those arising in later life usually do so after a frightening event involving the phobic object, for example a swarm of bees leading to a bee phobia. These phobias starting in later life have a better prognosis, although there has been very little work done to study outcomes in any of the simple phobias.

Agoraphobia

Symptoms

- Anxiety in situations where escape is difficult
- Fear of specific situations, i.e. crowds, public transport, lifts
- Active avoidance of feared situation
- Reduced social functioning.

Management

- Behaviour therapy
- Group therapy

- Drugs such as the antidepressants or (in the short term) benzodiazepines may be useful as adjuncts.

Agoraphobia affects about 0.3 per cent of the population and is twice as common in women. It usually starts in the mid-twenties and the first episode almost always involves the person experiencing a panic attack in a situation such as a crowded supermarket, or waiting for a bus. They will either seek help at hospital because of the intensity of their symptoms or will go home. Avoidance behaviour reinforces the phobia and in the most severe cases the individual will become confined to the home. If the agoraphobia has been present for a year it is usual for it to continue for at least five years; untreated it can become a chronic disabling condition.

Social phobia

Symptoms

- Extreme fear of social situations
- Fear of humiliation
- Fear of negative evaluation by others
- Avoidance behaviour
- Anticipatory anxiety
- Recognition of the irrational nature of the symptoms.

Management

- Behaviour therapy
- CBT
- Drugs such as moclobemide, SSRIs and beta blockers have a place.

Social phobia affects about 2.5 per cent of the population and is equally common in men and women. It usually occurs in late adolescence when many young people are concerned about the impression they are making on those around them. Symptoms usually improve in the mid-thirties. Many more people seek help for social phobia as opposed to simple phobias. Treatment can be quite successful, as these are usually a well-motivated group of clients although it is often long term. This phobia is likely to be seen in coaching, as it is the type of behaviour that will make a person underachieve.

Stress

Stress is likely to be seen quite commonly in coaching and other work-related situations. It is distressing for the client and will impair functioning in all aspects of life. It is important to have a knowledge and understanding of normal stress reactions to help the client and to prevent it from becoming an abnormal reaction. This can be done with sympathy to reduce the emotional distress, with help to develop more effective coping strategies, with encouragement to recall and talk about the event and with help and support with residual problems such as disability.

Normal reactions to stress involve anxiety and depression and a psychological response that reduces the unpleasant affects to tolerable levels. The responses involve both coping strategies and defensive mechanisms.

Adaptive coping strategies

- Avoidance
- Working through the problem
- Coming to terms with the situation.

Maladaptive coping strategies

- Excessive use of alcohol or drugs
- Histrionic or aggressive behaviour
- Deliberate self-harm.

Common defence mechanisms

- Regression to an earlier age often of dependence on others
- Repression of emotions or memory
- Denial of stress, which is particularly common in terminal illness
- Displacement of emotion onto another, for example blaming the doctor for the recent death of a loved one.

Less common defence mechanisms

- Rationalisation – the provision of a false but acceptable explanation
- Sublimation of impulses to alternative, more acceptable channels
- Projection of one's feelings onto others, making your own more acceptable
- Identification with another, particularly common in bereavement.

Management

- Reduce emotion with sympathetic listening
- Encourage recall and working through the event by talking
- Reassure that time is a great healer
- Problem solve in order to prevent recurrence and deal with residual disability
- Identify social support
- Introduce simple relaxation methods
- Occasionally short-term benzodiazepines.

Abnormal reactions to stressful situations

Acute stress disorder following a sudden intense stressor lasts at most a few days and is not an exacerbation of an existing psychiatric condition. The emotional response is excessive to the degree of stress and there may be panic attacks and generalised anxiety. Coping and defence mechanisms will be extreme and strong denial is common. Management of this reaction is the same as for any stressful situation, with sympathy, encouragement, recall and ongoing support. Time will be a great healer in these cases and the outcome is generally very good.

Post-traumatic stress disorder

Post-traumatic stress disorder (PTSD) follows very intense stressors, is prolonged and is associated with increased arousal, avoidance behaviour and flashbacks to the original event (see below). It usually develops 3–6 months after the event and the young, the elderly and those with a previous psychiatric illness are particularly vulnerable. A group of people experiencing the same intense stressor such as a major disaster will not all respond in the same way, and twin studies have suggested that there is at least some genetic predisposition to developing PTSD. This is often a chronic disorder and about half of those experiencing it will recover within five years. It is very difficult to treat and referral to an expert in the field is essential. In general, therapy involving recall and working through the emotions associated with the event will be employed. There is weak evidence for the use of medication although some SSRIs have been used.

Symptoms of PTSD

- Flashbacks of the original event
- Avoidance of anything that acts as a reminder of the event
- Amnesia about important aspects
- Intense arousal and anxiety on exposure to trauma cues
- Depression and irritability
- Social withdrawal
- Impaired concentration and memory
- Disturbed sleep.

Adjustment disorder

Adjustment disorder follows life changes. It is prolonged but does not meet the criteria for a specific psychiatric condition such as depression. The distress felt by the client is greater, in a subjective way, than would be anticipated. There is accompanying impairment of social functioning and it occurs within 1–3 months of the life change. It is a reaction most likely to occur after divorce, serious illness, retirement, leaving home and similar life changes. It generally lasts a few weeks and rarely longer than six months. Treatment is aimed at overcoming avoidance and denial and usually involves anxiety management and a problem-solving approach.

Problem solving

- Define and list the problems
- Choose a problem for action
- List alternative courses of action
- Evaluate the course of action and choose the best
- Try it
- Evaluate the results.

Summary

Anxiety and anxiety-related problems are relatively common and unlike some of the more severe mental health problems, most people affected will be in the workplace and leading relatively normal lives. Hopefully the chapter has given a few pointers on how to manage a situation and when to seek help. Basic commonsense and good listening skills have a therapeutic role in enabling many clients to overcome their difficulties and improve their functioning.

15

Addiction and dependence

Substance misuse is widespread and many individuals will have a problem with more than one substance. Presentation and management are remarkably similar for all prescribed or illicit drugs and alcohol. Additionally, there is a large hidden population whose dependence is not recognised either by themselves or others. Most of the treatment techniques available can help people who experience problems with alcohol or drugs but who do not yet meet the criteria for dependence.

Alcohol

Consumption of alcohol is socially acceptable and only about 10 per cent of the population are teetotal. Consumption doubled between 1950 and 1980 and there are an estimated 33,000 premature deaths as a result of excess alcohol intake in the UK each year.

At-risk consumption is defined as being greater than 28 units weekly for men and 21 units for women. At least 28 per cent of men exceed this 'safe' level, and 11 per cent of women. Recognition is particularly difficult in teenagers, the elderly and doctors. The old joke about the definition of an alcoholic being someone that drinks more than their doctor has some truth as in half the doctors referred to the General Medical Council with health difficulties, alcohol is the problem.

Problem drinking occurs in 1–2 per cent of the population and the level of consumption causes serious problems to the drinker, their family and to society. Alcohol consumption contributes to 1 in 3 divorces, 30 per cent of fatal road traffic accidents and 80 per cent of suicides.

Alcohol dependence affects about 200,000 people in the UK. It is a psychological syndrome generally seen after several years of misuse. It is diagnosed if at least three of the symptoms listed below have been present in the previous year.

Dependence

- A strong desire to take the substance
- Difficulty in controlling use
- Withdrawal syndrome (see below)
- Tolerance so that higher amounts are needed to achieve the same effect
- Self-neglect
- Persistent use despite suffering harm from it.

Alcohol withdrawal syndrome

- Restlessness
- Sweating
- Nausea and vomiting
- Anxiety
- High blood pressure
- Rapid heart rate
- Epileptic seizures
- Delirium tremens (severe disorientation, confusion, hallucinations, loss of consciousness)
- Ultimately death.

Presentation of an alcohol problem can be social, medical or psychiatric. Given the prevalence of the problem, coaches are likely to meet this and need to have some advice and help available for their clients.

Detection of an alcohol problem can be improved by using the CAGE questionnaire:

- Have you ever felt you should **C**ut down on your drinking?
- Have people **A**nnoyed you by criticising your drinking?
- Have you ever felt **G**uilty about your drinking?

- Have you ever had an **E**ye-opener drink first thing in the morning to steady your nerves or get rid of a hangover?

Two positive answers suggest an alcohol problem and your client may well need to address this to achieve their goals.

Table 15.1 Signs of alcohol problems

Social presentation	Medical presentation	Psychiatric presentation
• Marital problems • Financial problems • Public drunkenness • Aggression • Prosecutions; particularly for driving offences	• Liver disease • High blood pressure • Enlarged heart • Nerve damage • Bleeding from stomach • Some cancers	• Depression • Anxiety • Impotence • Hallucinations • Personality change

Management

About a third of people who seriously misuse alcohol will recover without any professional help.

Brief intervention and motivational interviewing aimed at assessing alcohol consumption, providing information about the effects and giving advice on reducing intake are very effective. This can be backed up with advice about the voluntary organisations that provide help with alcohol problems. Alcoholics Anonymous is the best-known organisation and others may be available locally; the client's doctor and the telephone directory will have contact details.

For some, controlled drinking is a reasonable option, when the amount drunk is reduced to safe levels and maintained there. However, abstinence is recommended if there is established dependence, previous failure of controlled drinking, or if there is physical damage such as cirrhosis. Relapse is very common and relapse prevention is an important strategy to develop. Relapses should be seen as opportunities to learn and not as failures, with positive reinforcement of what has been gained. Structured problem solving can be used to identify triggers that led to the relapse and develop strategies to deal with the issues rather than turning back to alcohol.

Additional support, particularly for those who experience withdrawal phenomena, is available in the first instance from the general practitioner. The general practitioner will also be able to access help from the mental health services. Community detoxification and in-patient rehabilitation are available through these sources. It has to be said that treatment for alcohol problems is patchy, under-resourced and often a struggle to access. It is easier to get treatment for a heroin problem than for an alcohol problem.

Drugs

At least 30 per cent of the population will have used illicit drugs at some time and the misuse of prescribed drugs is very common. Whilst all the drugs used remain illegal there are areas of social acceptability, particularly around cannabis use, and it is difficult to predict who will develop a problem drug habit.

Risk factors for problem drug use

- Age (late teens and early twenties)
- Peer group use
- Local cost and availability of drugs
- Local controls and sanctions on use
- Disordered lifestyle
- Personal vulnerability.

Dependence is defined in the same way as for alcohol (see above). Withdrawal varies depending on the type of substance being misused. Heroin withdrawal has a classic appearance of dilated pupils, yawning, vomiting, diarrhoea, muscle cramps, insomnia and excess salivation. However, not all addicts going 'cold turkey' will necessarily be severely affected.

Problem drug use is much more likely to be encountered in a coaching partnership where true dependence and withdrawal are not present but the regular use of drugs in the recreational setting affects performance, mood and functioning.

Commonly misused drugs

* Benzodiazepines
* Opioids (e.g. heroin)
* Amphetamines
* Cocaine (including crack cocaine)
* Ecstasy
* Volatile substances (e.g. glues)
* Cannabis.

Whilst the number of addicts using heroin continues to rise, the number injecting the drug is falling. Injecting is potentially very harmful and is responsible for most of the deaths among addicts. Historically, white heroin is only suitable for injection whilst brown heroin can be sniffed, eaten, smoked or injected. Brown heroin became available in the UK in the early 1970s and this along with a wider availability of health education aimed at the vulnerable population is responsible for the reduction in harmful injecting. In some parts of the world, white heroin remains the only form available. Heroin use is destructive and will not be commonly encountered in the coaching situation although there are a small number of 'stable' users who manage a normal life.

Crack is cocaine in its base form; it is bought as a 'rock' and smoked for its intense and rapid psychoactive effect. The 'rush' is felt within seconds, peaks at 1–5 minutes and wears off in 15 minutes. It is very addictive and cravings are severe. However, there are a group of people who use crack only intermittently and this may well affect their functioning in both work and social circumstances.

Weekend use of the other psychoactive drugs is believed to involve a large population, most of whom are not known to the drug services, but may well be encountered by the coach. The symptoms of withdrawal from cocaine after a weekend's use include lethargy and fatigue, increased appetite, insomnia and unpleasant dreams. Chronic intoxication with psychoactive drugs often leads to a poor work record and failure in relationships.

Management

This is similar to the management of problem drinking and dependence. A fair few people will not require professional help, but if the use of drugs is sufficient to cause withdrawal phenomena, referral to the general practitioner is advisable. Brief intervention aimed at setting attainable goals will help the majority of people. Narcotics Anonymous is a useful voluntary organisation and will help both the drug misuser and the family members. Withdrawal from opioids is usually a long and difficult path requiring specialist help and intervention.

Summary

People with addiction and dependence problems are likely to be met by those in professional relationships, be that coach, mentor, manager or human resource professional. Even more likely are people who are engaged in at-risk behaviour with both alcohol and drugs. Tackling the problem will depend on how ready the client is to change their behaviour; if they are at the pre-contemplative stage they will not consider change and coercing them into treatment will end in failure. Once they are aware of the problem and are contemplating change then offering a route to appropriate care is likely to be more effective.

16

Disabilities

Disabilities may be physical, intellectual or a mixture of the two. The coach is likely to meet a variety of disabilities in their practice and with disability discrimination law it is to be hoped that the workplace will become increasingly open to those with such difficulties. The commonest disability in the developed world is deafness. Some disabilities are diminishing with improved diagnosis and medical care, whilst others such as autism are apparently increasing. This chapter cannot explore all areas of disability but will concentrate on those that are most likely to impinge on the coaching relationship. The best source of information about the effects of disability, particularly physical disability, is the client themselves and the coach should explore the impact this has had on their client's life and the possible ways forward with them. Sensitive enquiry is not intrusive and will enhance the coaching relationship.

The central feature of learning difficulties is intellectual impairment with concurrent deficits and impairments in adaptive behaviour, taking into account the person's age (Definition DSM-IV, American Psychiatric Association 1994). Intellectual ability varies from mild impairment (IQ 50–70) to profound learning difficulties usually associated with physical disability. There are also a group of disorders that impair functioning but with normal intellectual ability such as dyslexia, which will be mentioned briefly.

The average general practitioner with a list of 2,000 patients will have 6–8 people with learning difficulties; only 1–2 of these will have severe difficulties. The person with mild learning difficulties (IQ 50–70) is capable of work and will benefit from appropriate training. However, simple intellectual ability does not tell the whole story and the impairment in adaptive behaviour may interfere considerably with the person's ability to function in the workplace and social environment. This is particularly well demonstrated in individuals with autistic spectrum disorder, which will be discussed below.

Down's syndrome

This is the commonest of the conditions causing learning difficulties, affecting 1 in every 600–700 births. It is due to a condition called Trisomy 21, which is an abnormality in the chromosomes (chromosomes are normally in pairs and trisomy is a condition where three chromosomes occur rather than the normal two). There is no known treatment. It is associated with a typical facial appearance and the learning difficulties can cover the entire spectrum from mild to severe. There are also a number of physical problems that may occur, such as heart abnormalities. Individuals with Down's syndrome are usually affectionate and easygoing, they rarely exhibit problematic behaviours and are often well integrated in the community. Those with mild intellectual impairment will usually go to mainstream schools, achieve success in public exams and should expect gainful employment. They will learn in a normal way albeit slowly and coaching could be highly effective with them. Their cheerful nature makes them very popular with colleagues. It is important to recognise that many people with Down's syndrome have very significant problems but these are unlikely to be involved in a coaching situation. In addition, about 10 per cent of those with Down's syndrome may have a dual diagnosis of autistic spectrum disorder.

Autistic spectrum disorder (ASD)
(Including Asperger's syndrome)

This is a complex developmental disorder that affects the way a person communicates and relates to people around them. It is believed to affect 500,000 people in the UK and is four times more common in males than females. Intellectual ability ranges from severe learning difficulties to above-average intelligence, but the impairment in adaptive behaviour will make the world a bewildering place even for those latter individuals. The cause of autism is not known, it is probably a combination of genetic factors and other influences on brain development. It is a lifelong condition which can be ameliorated by appropriate education and training. There is no known cure but many 'miracles' have been touted over the years and parents have been offered numerous treatments and false hopes from a variety of sources.

Asperger's syndrome is also known as 'high functioning autism' and describes people with normal or above-average intelligence. It occurs nine times more commonly in men than women. The diagnosis of Asperger's syndrome is often delayed and we are seeing increasing numbers of young men in their twenties and thirties presenting with the problem. Depression is more common in affected individuals and is often the first symptom presented to professionals.

Coaches are highly likely to find themselves confronted with an individual with this pattern of behaviour even if there is no solid diagnosis. The person will often be described by colleagues as 'odd', they will be a loner and unsure of social situations. People with ASD do not shun friendship; they simply do not understand the social cues to establish a relationship. They will also find apparently normal situations disturbing and stressful and may react by walking away or engaging in a repetitive behaviour to lower their anxiety. An example of this would be the hard-working computer programmer who, when called to a department meeting to discuss next month's work schedule, sits clicking his pen in and out until he abruptly leaves, muttering about needing the toilet. Alternatively, he may talk too much with an odd, very literal speech, not recognising social cues in a group setting and failing to understand many of the nuances in everyday social interactions. Working with someone with ASD is not easy; it is important to recognise their difference and to work around it. Standard behavioural techniques may not suffice and further up-to-date help and advice can be sought from specialist autistic agencies.

Cerebral palsy

Cerebral palsy comprises a conglomerate of non-progressive motor disabilities and affects about 2 per 1,000 births in most of the developed world. Visual disturbance, impaired hearing, speech disturbance and epilepsy are all common. Learning difficulties occur in 30–40 per cent of affected individuals. The commonest error that the public make with regard to this condition is assuming that those with speech disturbance have learning difficulties. Whilst those with cerebral palsy are subject to the whole range of mental health problems and can also have a dual diagnosis with autistic spectrum disorder the coach should be able to work well with a motivated person with cerebral palsy.

Attention deficit hyperactivity disorder (ADHD)

This is a somewhat controversial topic. The incidence varies widely depending on the criteria used to make the diagnosis but is generally accepted at 3–5 per cent of school-age children with a marked male preponderance. In parts of the world, particularly the US, the incidence is rising rapidly. There are polarised views on treatment and the duration of the illness. The overactivity and other symptoms seem to diminish in early adulthood and persistence into adult life is uncommon. Drug treatment is often with stimulant substances such as Dexamphetamine (Dexadrine) or Methylphenidate (Ritalin), both of which can be abused in the community and are usually supplied with specific controlled drug legislation. Parents may report a complete transformation in their child's behaviour. Others feel that powerful stimulants with recognised side effects should not be given to children.

The stimulant drugs work by improving concentration and reducing impulsivity and restlessness. The effects of the drug occur within one hour of ingestion and the duration is about 3–4 hours although individuals vary enormously in their response.

From the coach's point of view, a new diagnosis of ADHD in adulthood is still so rare that it doesn't warrant mention but working with an individual who has an established diagnosis could present some challenges. Deterioration in functioning may be a consequence of inadequate medication or incorrect timing of medication, as some people will experience a marked deterioration as the drug wears off. The help of an experienced physician is needed and if the coach is suspicious that a problem exists they should point their client in the right direction. However, the pitfall for the coach is to assume that the ADHD is the cause of impaired functioning when a mood disorder is to blame. Depression is all too common (see Chapter 13) and those with ADHD are at as much risk as the rest of the population.

Signs of ADHD include:

- Attention problems
- Impulsive behaviour
- Being disorganised
- Restlessness
- Emotional instability.

Dyslexia

This is a neurological disorder causing difficulties with reading, writing, spelling and understanding text. It is not a learning difficulty as there is no impairment in intelligence. The diagnosis appears to be increasing but this may well represent better recognition in the early years at school. Making the diagnosis is very beneficial as appropriate teaching can minimise the impact it has on the person's functioning and brings extra support, such as note taking in lectures and help whilst taking exams. There are undoubtedly adults with undiagnosed dyslexia who may be struggling in their work life because of an unrecognised problem. The dyslexic may well have an excellent vocabulary but be unable to spell the words they use or produce an adequate report for the boss. Assessment by an appropriately trained educational psychologist and then adequate support will produce enormous benefits.

Dyspraxia

This is a neurological disorder that causes problems with coordination and movement. It ranges from those profoundly affected and unable to coordinate even simple tasks such as protruding the tongue to those individuals described as 'always clumsy'. There is no specific treatment and, for the coach, identification enables the energies to be concentrated on living with the disorder and lessening its impact on the client and those around them.

Summary

The coach should not be afraid of disability and must not make assumptions about a person's ability to benefit from coaching on a false premise. They also need to be aware of the possibility of a diagnosis such as Asperger's syndrome and the impact that might have on functioning.

17

Psychosis and personality disorders

This chapter will look at the most serious group of mental illnesses and the influence of personality on functioning. Bipolar affective disorder, historically known as manic depressive illness, is included due to the similarities of behaviours and the severity of this disease.

Psychotic illness

Psychotic illness is, thankfully, quite rare when compared to depression but attracts a great deal of media attention. Headline news that someone just released from a psychiatric institution has committed a random murder is enough to make anyone afraid. However, most patients, even when seriously unwell with psychosis, are not a substantial danger and during periods of calm represent little threat. There are warning signs that the client may pose a danger either to themselves or the coach and these will be explored.

There are four groups of illness that fall into this category and differentiating between them depends predominantly on the duration and extent of symptoms.

Psychotic disorders

- Schizophrenia
- Acute and transient psychotic disorder
- Schizoaffective disorder
- Persistent delusional disorder.

Symptoms and signs

- Hallucinations (seeing, hearing, smelling, sensing or tasting things that others are not aware of).
- Delusions (false beliefs held against all evidence, and outside the cultural beliefs of the individual, e.g. believing oneself to be God).
- Thought disturbance (believing that thoughts are being inserted or withdrawn from the mind, being broadcast to others or being echoed in the mind).
- Disordered thinking (giving incoherent or irrelevant speech).
- Negative symptoms (extreme apathy, lack of speech, disturbed social functioning).

Schizophrenia

Schizophrenia affects about 1 in 100 individuals, equally distributed between men and women. It usually presents between the ages of 15–25 years, with men usually presenting earlier. There is a period that precedes the characteristic manifestations of the acute, fully developed illness, which is known as the prodromal phase. Expected signs would include: social withdrawal, irritability, odd beliefs and some odd behaviour, such as laughing inappropriately. The duration of this phase is anything from a few weeks to many months, the longer it goes on the worse the prognosis is for future functioning.

The active phase follows and will have evidence of all the psychotic symptoms detailed above. It is during this phase that most people will present to the medical professional for treatment. With medication the active phase can usually be brought under control (see Chapter 20). Untreated, the active phase may resolve or continue indefinitely. It is a very distressing time for all involved and prompt treatment may literally save lives.

Management of the active phase

1 Ensure the safety of the individual and others.
2 Reduce the symptoms of psychosis and disturbed behaviour.

3 Build a therapeutic relationship with the individual and carers.
4 Have a coordinated management plan to aid recovery.

Most people have some residual disability, although the extent of impairment is variable. Some people will only have a single acute episode and then function remarkably well. About 25 per cent of people will experience complete recovery, 40 per cent will experience recurrent active phases of illness with some residual disability between episodes and the remaining 35 per cent will be chronically disabled requiring a great deal of social support.

The acute phase of schizophrenia, especially the first episode, is terrifying and confusing both for the individual and those around them. Assessing risk is essential although the greatest risk is to the individual themselves. It is estimated that 10 per cent of people with schizophrenia will have committed suicide within five years of the onset of the illness. This is an area of mental health that needs immediate professional input and should be reported at once to those who can influence the individual. Sadly, for many there is no insight that their terrifying thoughts are part of an illness and early help may have to be under an appropriate legal framework (such as the 1983 Mental Health Act in the UK).

Harm to others can be a result of hallucinatory voices commanding the person to act in that way. Additionally, paranoid ideas can lead the person with schizophrenia to feel persecuted by an individual or organisation and they may decide to take matters into their own hands to stop the persecution.

Risk factors for harm to others

- Blaming an individual or group for their problems
- Believing the persecutor should be punished
- Irresistible 'voices' demanding violent behaviour
- A plan of action to respond to the above beliefs
- The necessary skills to carry out their plan
- Evidence of impulsive behaviour.

Acute and transient psychotic disorder

Acute and transient psychotic disorder is a diagnosis made when the psychotic symptoms are present for less than one month. The illness is the same as the active phase of schizophrenia but with a rapid onset over two weeks, no prodromal phase and rapid resolution. It is usually precipitated by an acute and stressful life event. It occurs most commonly in adolescence and early adulthood, recovery is usually complete and happens within 2–3 months. Treatment includes the antipsychotic drugs, structured problem solving and stress management.

Schizoaffective disorder

Schizoaffective disorder is an illness characterised by the presence of schizophrenic symptoms and affective symptoms, changes in mood at odds with what would be expected. Affective symptoms are either depressive or manic (see below for a description of bipolar affective disorder). The incidence is less than that for schizophrenia; it affects predominantly the young with a family history of affective illness and there is little or no prodromal phase. The illness usually comes on very quickly and particularly with manic features has a good prognosis, recovery occurring within weeks. However, some individuals will have residual disability, or may take much longer to recover, particularly if there are marked depressive features. Lithium is often an effective treatment when used in conjunction with antipsychotic therapies.

Persistent delusional disorder

Persistent delusional disorder is characterised by the presence of a single delusion without hallucinations or disturbance of behaviour. The delusion may be persecutory, grandiose, hypochondriacal (a false belief about illness) or morbid jealousy. Individuals may function very well in most areas of their lives and only reveal the delusion under specific circumstances. The author (CB) well remembers one of the first patients she saw in psychiatric outpatients who was a smart, articulate personal assistant to the MD of a

multinational company. It was only when her usual practitioner joined the consultation and pressed the right
buttons that her firm belief that the devil lived in her head
came out!

Treatment of this condition depends on how intrusive
the symptoms are and will include both medication and
structured problem solving.

Schizoid personality disorder could be confused with
persistent delusional disorder. The personality disorders are
considered in more depth below but the major diagnostic
difference is that the personality disorder presents as a
chronic disorder of at least two years' duration. The individual will have eccentric and odd behaviour, often with
social withdrawal. Whilst they may have psychotic symptoms
they will be transient, lasting only hours or days.

Bipolar affective disorder (manic depressive illness)

In an academic textbook of psychiatry bipolar affective disorder would be in the chapter with the other disorders of
mood such as depression. The decision to place bipolar disorder here is based on the severity of the illness and its relative rarity. It affects about 1 per cent of the population and
both sexes equally. Generally it presents before the age of 30
but delays in diagnosis are not uncommon. It is characterised by cyclical mood disturbance with mania, depression or
a mixture of the two. The most frequent presentation is of
episodes of mania or depression with complete remission in
between. The symptoms of depression have been dealt with
in Chapter 13 and those of mania are detailed below.

Symptoms of mania

- Elevated mood
- Grandiosity
- Increased activity
- Rapid, pressured, often unintelligible speech
- Flights of ideas where the mind races around a whole host
  of loosely connected ideas
- Disinhibited sexual activity

- Impaired judgement and impulsive behaviour
- Decreased need for sleep
- Increased creativity
- Psychotic symptoms such as delusions and hallucinations.

Manic episodes usually have an abrupt onset and untreated can last for six months. The poor judgement associated with these episodes can lead to very serious consequences. Accidents, sometimes leading to death, aggressive behaviour and marked impairment in social and occupational functioning take a considerable toll on the individual and those around them. The abrupt onset can be startling and when your normally cooperative colleague buys a new fast car and drives you to the business meeting at excessive speed accompanied by staccato speech and gesturing, then becomes very angry when you remonstrate with them, you are entitled to be anxious. The individual rarely has any insight that their behaviour is a problem and they are often frightening in the extreme. Treatment in the acute phase is almost always against the person's free will, as they do not feel they are ill. History has many examples of creative individuals with a bizarre streak who probably had bipolar affective disorder (van Gogh being one of them).

Depressive episodes usually have a more gradual onset, last longer and fade more slowly than the manic episodes. The depth of the individual's despair puts them at a real risk of suicide and social functioning can be virtually impossible.

This is a chronic disorder with an unpredictable course but the periods of depression tend to occur more frequently and with increasing regularity as the person ages. Treatment of the acute phase is with the antipsychotic drugs, mood stabilisers and antidepressants. Long-term use of the mood stabilisers such as Lithium can have enormous benefit in terms of reducing periods of illness. Unfortunately as the person's mood starts to elevate towards mania they feel so well that they stop taking the medication! Hospitalisation is almost always necessary during manic episodes because even if frankly psychotic symptoms are not present the person has no insight into their dangerous behaviour.

Assessment of risk to others

- Psychotic symptoms demonstrating the same risks as detailed on p. 215
- Aggressive, arrogant or insensitive behaviour
- Promiscuous or sexually inappropriate behaviour
- Poor judgement leading to damaging social or business decisions.

The manic phase of this illness is one of the most frightening and potentially dangerous illnesses in psychiatry. The person with schizophrenia is bizarre and withdrawn, risk is easier to assess and change is more gradual. The apathy often associated with schizophrenic illness makes it difficult for the individual to achieve anything. Appearances can be deceptive in bipolar disorder. A person with a manic illness can present as warm, fun loving and enthusiastic. However, their behaviour will deteriorate rapidly and they have a lot of energy to carry out their plans. Urgent help needs to be found. The lack of insight into their illness precludes any help from rational argument or discussion, obstructing them could lead to rapidly escalating violence.

Personality disorders

Everyone has personality. It represents a pattern of thinking and behaviour that persists across time and situations and is influenced by both heredity and the environment. Aside from this it represents a complex and controversial area.

Definitions abound. Presentation is along a continuum with no clear cut-off about what is 'normal' or 'abnormal' and treatment is complex and often ineffective. The ICD-10 definition is: 'an extreme deviation from the way an average person in a particular culture perceives, thinks, feels and relates to others' (WHO 1994). The behaviour must be enduring and pervasive and not a reaction to a particular event. Increasing age blunts the problems associated with personality and therapy is usually aimed at finding a way of life that offers less conflict with the problematic personality. Governments and the police force have an interest in those with a personality that tends to violence and there can be

conflict between the psychiatric services and other author-
ities on management of these individuals. No one yet has the
answer to this dilemma.

Additionally, there are instances where a 'personality
disorder' can benefit the individual and society. The ball-
sport player who repeatedly practises goal scoring until they
are almost infallible is an enormous asset to the team, but
their behaviour is very obsessional and well outside 'normal'
behaviour.

Personality types

- Paranoid
- Withdrawn
- Violent
- Antisocial
- Impulsive
- Histrionic
- Dependent
- Obsessional
- Passive-aggressive.

Paranoid personality types can vary from mildly suspicious
to extremely delusional. They can be recognised by their
excessive concern for confidentiality, beliefs of persecution,
hostility and often, repeated terminations of employment.

Withdrawn personality types include those with a schizoid personality and an anxious personality. These people
usually function well in employment which allows them to
keep themselves to themselves but become anxious in social
settings and appear aloof and reserved. The anxious person
wants to relate to others but feels they may be rejected. Time
will often see a great improvement in this person's ability to
cope. The schizoid personality has little interest in people
and will remain aloof.

Violent and antisocial personality types include those
described as sociopathic or psychopathic and the term used
varies depending on whether a legal or medical definition is
being applied. These individuals have poor control of
aggression. The coach would be well advised to steer well
clear of this personality for obvious reasons.

Impulsive personality types may also be prone to angry outbursts but this is often directed at themselves. In most psychiatric literature this is referred to as borderline personality disorder. These individuals are emotionally unstable, demonstrating sudden mood swings and impulsive actions without consideration of the consequences. Their self-image is unclear and disturbed with repeated emotional crises particularly in relationships. There is evidence that long-term psychotherapy with a skilled practitioner can be helpful to these people.

Histrionic personality types present as very dramatic, even the most mundane information being presented in a lively way. They will set out to capture the audience's attention, appear self-centred and may have inappropriate sexually seductive behaviour. This personality type diminishes in its extent with increasing maturity and age. The single most important aspect of working with these individuals is to not reward the behaviour with undue attention.

Dependent personality types avoid decision making and have a strong need for reassurance. They will seek frequent contact with the coach and exhibit excessive thankfulness for help. It is essential to set clear boundaries and have achievable goals for the individual, whilst avoiding the pitfall of making decisions for them. The coach should turn the behaviour of this personality type to their advantage by, for example, acknowledging how well the individual gets on with them and then suggesting an independent task they might undertake.

Obsessive personality types are perfectionists, conscientious and scrupulous. They would seem the ideal employee if it weren't for their excessive cautiousness, preoccupation with detail and need for everyone to conform to their way of doing things. The coach should aim to divert their obsessive traits into more useful tasks and encourage them to relax.

Passive-aggressive personality types are the classic 'yes, but' person. They will arrive late for appointments, challenge the coach and blame everyone else for any problems that have arisen. It is unlikely they will complete tasks set them and will resent any demands put on them. It is vital to set consistent limits and be firm in applying them to these individuals. For example after the first late arrival set a clear time that you are prepared to wait for and stick to it.

There are emerging classifications in personality disorder and differences in diagnosis and management around the world. The descriptions given above have described personality types rather than single definitions and in general the newer diagnoses can fit into one of the above. An example of this is the narcissistic personality who fits into the antisocial category. This type is increasingly recognised in the US but is little diagnosed across Europe. The individual cares only for themselves, is arrogant and has a sense of entitlement to all they wish for. They are sensitive to perceived slights and this can result in rage and a desire for revenge. They have little attachment to values and are potentially very dangerous to work with. Roy Lubit has some useful descriptions of this personality type, and many others, in his book *Coping with Toxic Managers, Subordinates and other Difficult People* (Lubit 2004: 13).

It is beyond the scope of this text to offer individual support and advice on managing all the personality types as listed above but the coach will meet them all to some degree. The main aim should be to harness individual skills and reduce areas of conflict. Professional help for these people is highly specialised, complex and of variable effectiveness. A person's personality will determine how they respond to illness and life events. Recognition of this can help the coach get the best from an individual.

Summary

It is worth commenting on the personal safety of the coach and detailed below are tips for staying safe, particularly if feeling threatened:

- Never turn your back.
- Allow a safe escape route preferably for both you and the client. If the client feels cornered they are more likely to be violent.
- Offer the opportunity for the client to escape ('I can see this is difficult, we should stop for today.').

- Do not interrupt.
- Stay calm.
- Do not wrestle with the aggressive person.
- Adopt a non-threatening body posture with minimal eye contact.
- Keep the individual speaking rather than acting by using brief prompts.
- Escape as soon as a safe opportunity arises.

18

Eating disorders

Eating disorders should be more correctly termed 'dieting disorders' as they represent a disordered diet. The commonest disorder in the world these days is obesity although this is rarely considered a mental health problem. Obesity is associated with many physical problems such as osteo-arthritis, diabetes and heart disease. It also causes psychological problems as it can destroy a person's confidence and self-worth. It has been linked with poorer career prospects and other forms of discrimination. What distinguishes it from anorexia nervosa and bulimia nervosa is that many people who are obese lead active, full and normal lives. Those with an anorexia nervosa or bulimia have all got psychological problems and many will have associated physical problems.

Anorexia nervosa

A diagnosis of anorexia nervosa is made if:

- The Body Mass Index is 17.5 or less.
- Weight loss is self-induced.
- Body image is distorted with a morbid fear of fatness.
- Women experience a loss of periods and men a loss of libido. This is often associated with measurable bio-chemical abnormalities in blood chemistry.

The true extent of this disorder is difficult to determine, as most individuals will deny their symptoms. However, surveys have suggested a prevalence of 1–2 per cent amongst schoolgirls and female university students. It is far more common amongst girls than boys and typically presents in the middle teens although it has been seen in recent years amongst children as young as six years of age. It seldom presents above the age of 30 years. It is more common higher up the social scale, and can have a poor prognosis. Whilst up to 70 per cent may return to a normal weight with treatment, relapse is common, affecting up to 25 per cent and long-term follow-up suggests that as many as 1 in 5 will eventually die from the disorder.

Anorexia differs from normal dieting in several ways. Most dieters talk about their goals and tactics with friends and colleagues. In anorexia nervosa weight loss goals are constantly revised downwards, dieting is in isolation and is a solitary activity. Anorexics will also utilise other means to lose weight:

- Self-induced vomiting
- Laxative abuse
- Diuretic abuse
- Excessive exercise
- Appetite suppressants.

The client with anorexia nervosa will avoid social eating situations, will often take exercise over the lunch period, such as 'power walking' and will wear bulky concealing clothing. They will know in minute detail the calorie content of everything that might cross their lips and will maintain the most rigid weight it is possible to imagine; a few ounces of weight gain will reinforce all the anorexic behaviour. They will eat very slowly, consuming excessive amounts of water and leave the table frequently during meals. Prognosis is worse if onset is later; the duration of the illness is prolonged and has associated mental health problems or personality disorder.

Physical consequences of anorexia nervosa

- Sensitivity to cold
- Constipation
- Low blood pressure
- No menstrual periods

- Dental decay (due to vomiting and poor diet)
- Osteoporosis (bone thinning)
- Low potassium levels (due to vomiting and laxative abuse)
- Epilepsy
- Slow heart rate or heart arrhythmias
- Heart failure
- Abnormal growth hormone levels
- Death.

Treatment is aimed at realistic goal setting, with alternative coping strategies. Structured problem solving can be very beneficial. It needs a carefully structured environment, relaxation training and often assertiveness training. If the weight loss is extreme or very rapid, admission to hospital for feeding may be needed. There are no specific medications that have shown real benefit in the treatment of the mental health problem but treatment may be needed for the physical problems, such as calcium supplements to prevent bone fracture.

This is a difficult and highly specialised area of psychiatry and referral to an appropriately trained specialist is essential.

Bulimia nervosa

Bulimia nervosa is diagnosed if:

- An individual consumes large quantities of food in a short period of time, satisfying irresistible cravings and a preoccupation with food (binge eating).
- Compensatory weight loss behaviours occur. These include self-induced vomiting, purging, periodic starvation, excessive exercise and abuse of drugs that increase weight loss such as thyroid hormone or diuretics.
- The individual has a morbid fear of fatness, striving to achieve a weight that is below their optimum.

Most of this group are women, are often of normal weight and they usually have normal periods. Self-induced vomiting to control weight is remarkably common and has been estimated to affect up to 13 per cent of college students. This condition has only risen to prominence in recent years and its prognosis is not clear. Treatment seems to lead to recovery in up to 70 per cent of people affected, but untreated it may have a chronic course. Early recognition and treatment seems to vastly improve prognosis, although personality disorder, low self-esteem and impulsivity are features that suggest poor outcome. There has been a big increase in the presentation of people with bulimia nervosa since several prominent personalities 'came out' and confessed to suffering from it, the most notable probably being Diana, Princess of Wales.

Binge eating occurs on a daily basis and vast quantities of food may be consumed. The person reports a loss of self-control and will consume high fat and carbohydrate foods that would normally be avoided in a diet. The episodes usually occur in secret, often in the evening and at weekends. There are several physical consequences of this condition that are listed below.

Physical symptoms of bulimia nervosa

- Dental decay (due to vomiting)
- Swollen salivary glands, sometimes confused with mumps
- Irritable bowel syndrome
- Diarrhoea from laxative abuse
- Hoarse voice
- Fatigue
- Callused knuckles
- Headache
- Hair loss.

Given that many of these clients are of a normal weight and function well in a social setting, bulimia nervosa may not impinge on the coaching relationship. However, it is felt that the two disorders are along a continuum and bulimics may progress to more serious illness. Should a client confess to an eating disorder the coach should encourage them to seek help even if it is not impinging on the coaching. Management is aimed at restoring normal eating patterns and identifying and treating any underlying psychosocial problems. There is some evidence to support the use of Fluoxetine (Prozac) in the treatment of bulimia nervosa.

Summary

People with dieting disorders believe many dieting myths and it can take a long time to promote healthy eating.

If anorexia nervosa or bulimia is suspected, encourage the client to seek professional help. The warning signs are detailed below.

Anorexia nervosa

- Refusing to eat
- Obsessive calorie counting
- Leaving the table frequently
- Drinking a lot of water
- Playing with the food on the plate
- Preoccupation with food
- Eating in isolation
- Excessive thinness (often hidden by clothing).

Bulimia nervosa

- Disappearing to the toilet after a large meal
- Poor teeth
- Excessive comfort-eating with stressful events
- Cravings for particular foods, usually fattening foods.

19

Psychosexual problems

In no other area of human behaviour is there a wider range of normal functioning and it is often difficult to define what constitutes a problem. In general, if the person and their sexual partner do not consider that a problem exists then it probably doesn't. In a multicultural society the coach needs to be aware of different beliefs and attitudes towards sexual behaviour. It is not appropriate to impose personally held beliefs on someone from a different culture.

Sexual dysfunction

This describes impaired or dissatisfying sex. It is the commonest problem to present to clinicians. The causes of sexual dysfunction are listed below. It is obvious from this list that they are unlikely to impinge on the coach. However, if the client mentions them as a problem in the sessions the coach can offer reassurance that help is available and refer them onto an appropriate physician.

Common sexual dysfunctions

- Lack or loss of sexual desire
- Sexual aversion
- Lack of sexual enjoyment
- Failure of genital response
- Orgasmic dysfunction
- Premature ejaculation

- Nonorganic vaginismus (muscular spasm around the vagina making penetration impossible)
- Nonorganic dyspareunia (pain with sexual intercourse).

Psychological problems associated with homosexuality

Societies differ in their attitudes to homosexuality and many of these differences reflect the attitudes of the major religions. As the influence of religion on society varies, so are the attitudes modified. Only 1 per cent of men and 0.25 per cent of women report exclusively homosexual attraction. However, 6 per cent of men and 3 per cent of women report some homosexual experience and two-thirds of the population believe homosexuality is sometimes or always wrong. Bisexual behaviour is most common in adolescence following which most people settle into a permanent sexual role.

Homosexuality is not a psychiatric disorder but homosexuals can experience sexual and emotional problems as a consequence of their sexual preference.

Homosexual women present less frequently with psychosexual difficulties than men, and when they do it is usually with relationship problems such as jealousy or depression. Sexual intercourse is not an imperative in many lesbian relationships and many societies do not view two women living together as out of the ordinary. Encouraging a woman who expresses any difficulties around a lesbian relationship to seek help through counselling can be expected to achieve great benefit. Additionally, homosexual women married to a man can, not surprisingly, experience difficulties in their relationship with their husband and families and again should be encouraged to seek counselling.

Homosexual men present with four distinct problems:

1 Sexually inexperienced (usually young) men may present with homosexual thoughts and feelings but be unclear about their sexual orientation. Psychosexual counselling can help the individual decide how he would prefer to develop.
2 Other men may present having recognised that they are

predominantly homosexual but needing help and counselling about the implications this may have for their lives.
This needs to be in the context of their religious and
cultural beliefs. Self-help groups for homosexuals are
most beneficial for this group, no problem is unique and
someone will have been there before. They are mutually
supportive and local groups can usually be found on the
internet.

3 Established homosexuals may present with relationship
difficulties, becoming depressed and anxious. Advice and
help is needed around their emotional wellbeing and is the
same for all, their homosexuality is coincidental.

4 Health anxieties about AIDS and other sexually transmit-
ted diseases are justifiably common in sexually active
homosexuals and the client should be referred to the local
genitourinary medicine clinic for appropriate counselling
and investigation.

Gender problems

Disorders of gender identity are uncommon and there is
some confusion about the classification of these entities.
Transexualism is most commonly seen in men but it is very
rare. The person believes they are of the opposite sex to that
indicated by the external genitalia. They will seek medical
help to alter their appearance to that of the opposite sex and
will live as a member of that sex. For most men the feeling
that they are in the wrong body starts before puberty
although help is not sought until much later. They report no
erotic fantasies from cross-dressing and do not seek to
attract others into a homosexual relationship. The incidence
is less than 1:100,000 people.

The demands to alter their appearance will be made in
a persistent way, sometimes accompanied by threats of suicide or self-mutilation. These threats are carried through
in a significant number of cases. It has been reported that
as many as 16 per cent of transsexuals have attempted
suicide. No form of psychotherapy has been shown to alter
this determination to change sex and gender reassignment
is available in a few highly specialised centres. It is a long

process and requires a great deal of psychological support as well as surgery and hormone manipulation. In some countries the law has now recognised the position of a transsexual and allows the change of sex to be recorded on official documentation such as passports.

Transvestism or cross-dressing is a very different condition. Most women who cross-dress and imitate men are homosexual and not transsexual. The cross-dressing can vary from an occasional occurrence to permanently living in the clothes of the opposite sex. Most men who cross-dress are heterosexual although some are effeminate homosexuals. Cross-dressers often report sexual arousal as a consequence of their dress. The cross-dressing often starts around puberty and whilst initially concealed as just a few garments under masculine clothes can progress to full cross-dressing in public. Transvestism develops slowly from puberty and may represent a problem with sexual development. It tends to diminish with advancing age as sexual drive diminishes. If help is sought by an individual any chance of success is strongly influenced by the motivation to change. If a man is sent by his wife for treatment after she 'catches' him in her clothes, no progress will be made unless the man himself wishes to change.

Along with other sexual deviations, help is often only sought after the issue has been made public. It is important at the start to recognise what the aim of treatment is. Is it to improve the person's functioning and adjustment or is it to change the behaviour?

Counselling to help the person explore their feelings and the problems caused by the sexual practice and develop ways of lessening the impact on their life will improve functioning. If the aim is to bring about change then treatment is first aimed at any anxieties that impede normal social relationships followed by therapy to deal with sexual inadequacy.

Disorders of sexual preference

Sexual preference can be described as abnormal if most people in a society regard it as abnormal. Additionally, if the sexual preference is harmful to others or if the individual themselves suffers as a consequence of the variant behaviour it can be described as abnormal.

There are two principal categories that disorders of preference fall into: abnormalities of the sexual 'object' and disorders of the sexual act.

Abnormalities of the sexual object

* Fetishism describes the condition when an inanimate object is the preferred or only means of achieving sexual satisfaction. Predominantly affecting men, common objects are rubber garments and high-heeled shoes.
* Paedophilia is repeated sexual activity or the fantasy of such activity with pre-pubertal children. Again predominantly affecting men, it is likely that paedophilic fantasy is not uncommon given the ease with which pornographic material of this type can be obtained. However, exclusive paedophilic behaviour is relatively rare.

Disorders of the sexual act

* Exhibitionism involves the exposure of the genitalia to a stranger. Again predominantly a male problem, it can present in two ways. Either a man with an aggressive personality trait may expose an erect penis whilst masturbating and feels no guilt about it. Or a sexually inhibited individual will expose a flaccid penis and suffer a great deal of guilt after it.
* Voyeurism is observing others in the act of intercourse or whilst undressing. Most are heterosexual men with sexual inhibitions.
* Sadomasochism involves bondage and inflicting pain either on others (sadism) or receiving such stimulation (masochism). Mild forms of sadomasochism are common and indeed are regarded as a part of normal sexual activity. In some individuals, however, it is the most important source of sexual gratification and whilst it may be symbolic, causing little harm, there is the potential for serious injury or even death with the more extreme acts.

Autoerotic asphyxiation is a particularly deadly form of sadomasochism as it is often a solitary activity.

The management of disorders of sexual preference involves five steps:

1 Identifying the problem and its course.
2 Excluding associated mental health problems such as alcoholism, depression and mania. This is often indicated by a later onset of symptoms in middle age.
3 Assessing whether there is any normal sexual function.
4 Assessing the role the deviation plays in the person's life to allow for adaptive coping mechanisms when the behaviour is extinguished.
5 Assessing motivation for treatment as it is often sought after the deviant behaviour has become public knowledge and treatment success is unlikely if the person themselves has no desire to change.

Treatment involves a mix of counselling and education and success is variable.

Summary

In most coaching situations psychosexual problems are unlikely to be an issue. The coach needs to recognise the cultural setting in which they are present and also recognise that for many individuals the behaviour is not a problem that they want to solve. Should the client express a wish to seek help, referral to an appropriate clinician will bring benefits. If working in a team situation there may need to be discussion around the impact of the behaviour on team members. This is particularly true with cross-dressing and often an open discussion will reduce the fear or embarrassment that others may feel and allow the team to function effectively.

If the coach believes that the law is being broken or that others are at risk then the behaviour must be reported to an appropriate authority. The likeliest scenario in which this would occur is probably accessing paedophilic pornographic material via the internet.

20

Treatment choices

The choice of treatment for mental health problems falls into three areas: psychiatric medication, formal talking treatments and patience. Patience may not sound like a treatment choice, but many people will return to normal functioning given time with nothing more formal in the way of treatment than some reassurance, maybe rest and the support of friends and family. Allowing patients the choice of treatment is important in the less severe conditions. Some people will prefer a course of medication, some to spend time with a counsellor whilst others may choose to wait and see if things get better without formal treatment.

Knowledge of what treatment may be offered will prove useful to the coach, or other professional, when a client is being treated for a mental health problem. Some of the psychiatric medications may impair functioning and make any coaching difficult, whilst coaching a client who is also seeing a counsellor or psychotherapist has implications, as discussed in Chapter 4.

Psychiatric medication: its appropriate use and the common side effects

Drugs have radically altered the treatment of mental illness but, as with all medical treatments, are not without adverse effects. Deciding on drug treatment is like taking a set of kitchen scales and placing the benefits that might be gained from the medication on one side and the potential risks of the medication and the consequences of not taking it on the other. This is further complicated in clients at risk of suicide as many of the drugs used are dangerous in overdose. In some situations their coincidental side effects dictate the choice of drug. For instance Tricyclic antidepressants are sedating and can be used at night to relieve insomnia. They are also useful as an adjunct treatment in chronic pain management.

There is no convincing evidence that any groups of antidepressants are more efficacious than others. The choice of drug will be multifactorial and will depend on such things as previous response to medication, the need or otherwise for sedation, the lifestyle of the client and, as mentioned, the suicide risk. Sadly, the choice may also be influenced by cost as the older drugs and those off patent will usually be cheaper.

Recently there has been a lot of interest in 'natural' remedies and there is a growing body of evidence that Hypericum extract (St John's Wort) is as effective as other antidepressants in treating depression (Szegedi et al., 2005: 503–506). The usual dose is 900–1800mg daily in divided doses and the side effects are few. The most common side effects are dry mouth, fatigue and headache. It should also be remembered that Hypericum has significant interactions with other medication (such as the combined oral contraceptive pill) and it is advisable to check with the pharmacist about potential interactions if other tablets are being taken.

Presented in the tables that follow are some of the more common drugs used with their brand names and doses. Lists are provided of the more common side effects, although as has been explained above these side effects may be useful in their own way.

Tricyclic antidepressants

These are the 'older' drugs and are effective at treating depression as long as a therapeutic dose is used. Unfortunately, their side effects often limit the dose that can be administered and the dose remains sub-optimal and therefore ineffective. They are also very dangerous in overdose and must be used with caution or in a closely supervised setting if the client is at risk of suicide.

Table 20.1 **Tricyclic antidepressants: common drugs used**

Drug	Brand names	Daily dose range
amitriptyline	Lentizol, Tryptizol, etc.	100–300mg
dosulepin	Prothiaden	75–150mg
lofepramine	Gamanil	140–210mg
imipramine	Tofranil	100–300mg
clomipramine	Anafranil, Tranquax	100–250mg

Common side effects:

- Sedation
- Dry mouth
- Blurred vision
- Weight gain
- Constipation
- Sweating.

Less common but serious side effects:

- Acute urinary retention
- Erectile impotence
- Glaucoma
- Heart problems
- Postural drop in blood pressure leading to fainting and dizziness.

Selective serotonin reuptake inhibitor antidepressants (SSRIs) and related compounds

Newer drug compounds have been hailed by the drug companies and the psychiatric community as the answer to depression and the problem with tricyclics. They include such compounds as Prozac (an SSRI), Effexor (an SNRI) (selective serotonin and noradrenaline reuptake inhibitor) and Zispin (a noradrenergic and serotonergic enhancer). Problems are beginning to emerge with this group of drugs as well. Some have been implicated in an increased risk of suicide and agitation whilst some have demonstrated problems on their withdrawal. However, they are safer in overdose and are generally better tolerated allowing their use at optimal doses from the start of treatment.

The side effects differ for the different drugs and an individual will need specific information on what to expect depending on which they are taking. They are also used to treat a variety of other conditions such as anxiety, bulimia nervosa, panic disorder and obsessive compulsive disorder.

Table 20.2 SSRIs and related compounds: common drugs used

Drug	Brand name	Daily dose range
fluoxetine	Prozac	20–60mg
citalopram	Cipramil	10–40mg
paroxetine	Seroxat	10–50mg
sertraline	Lustral	50–200mg
venlafaxine	Effexor	75–225mg
reboxetine	Edronax	8–12mg
mirtazepine	Zispen	15–45mg

Common side effects:
- Nervousness and anxiety
- Sleep disturbance
- Nausea
- Diarrhoea
- Disturbed sexual function
- Loss of appetite and weight loss.

Less common but serious side effects:
- Fits
- Serotonin syndrome (see below)
- Haemorrhage
- Heart arrhythmias.

Serotonin syndrome
- Difficulty speaking

- Poor coordination
- Increased heart rate and blood pressure
- Mania
- Confusion
- Tremor.

Monoamine oxidase inhibitors (MAOIs) – antidepressants

Monoamine oxidase (MAO) is an enzyme found in the brain, and there are so-called irreversible and reversible inhibitors that are believed to work by blocking MAO-A in the brain. The term 'reversible' denotes those in which the action of the drug wears off in 12 hours, in the others it takes at least two weeks before the enzyme returns to normal function. This is particularly important as food and medicines containing amine products cause dangerous changes in blood pressure if taken in conjunction with MAOIs. A person taking this group of antidepressant will have a strict diet sheet excluding many products such as cheese, home-brewed beer and yeast extracts. Over the counter and herbal remedies may also be dangerous. Because of these strict restrictions and with the newer drugs available they are less commonly used and are generally only started by psychiatrists in patients who have not responded to other treatment.

Table 20.3 **MAOIs: common drugs used**

Drug	Brand name	Daily dose range
moclobemide – reversible	Manerix	300–600mg
phenelzine – irreversible	Nardil	15–45mg

Common side effects:

- Sleep disturbance
- Agitation
- Dizziness
- Weight gain
- Oedema.

Mood stabilisers

These are an interesting group of drugs that are being used increasingly commonly for a wider range of disorders. The first to be used was lithium, which is a metallic element found to have antimanic properties in 1949. The other drugs used are carbamazepine and sodium valproate, both of which are antiepileptic. Psychiatric uses of this group are in the treatment of acute mania, prophylaxis in bipolar effective disorder and recurrent depressive illness and as an adjunct treatment in acute depression.

Table 20.4 Mood stabilisers: common drugs used

Drug name	Brand name	Dose range
lithium carbonate	Priadel, Camcolit	500–2000mg
carbamazepine	Tegretol	400–1600mg
sodium valproate	Epilim	600–2400mg

Side effects of lithium:

- Nausea
- Diarrhoea
- Metallic taste
- Weight gain
- Difficulty concentrating
- Increased thirst
- Acne
- Underactive thyroid gland.

Side effects of carbamazepine:

- Nausea and vomiting
- Sedation
- Skin rashes
- Dizziness
- Ataxia.

Side effects of valproate:

- Nausea and vomiting
- Sedation

- Diarrhoea
- Hair loss
- Weight gain
- Memory loss.

Benzodiazepines

These well-known drugs may act as sedatives, anxiolytics, hypnotics and muscle relaxants. There are numerous types available and there is a roaring trade in their illicit use. They are extremely effective medications and their role in prescribed use depends on how long they stay active in the body (the half life), the length of time it takes to produce the desired effect and their potency. They, are of course, all addictive and this gives them their street value.

Table 20.5 Benzodiazepines: common drugs used

Drug name	Brand name
chlordiazepoxide	Librium
diazepam	Valium
flunitrazepam	Rohypnol
flurazepam	Dalmane
lorazepam	Ativan
nitrazepam	Mogadon
temazepam	Temazepam

Side effects:

- Addiction
- Sedation
- Ataxia
- Disinhibition
- Respiratory depression
- Seizure (on abrupt withdrawal after prolonged use).

There are some newer non-benzodiazepine alternatives such as Zopiclone (used for night sedation) but they still have similar problems to the classic benzodiazepines and need to be used with caution.

Antipsychotic medication

This group of treatments can be broadly grouped into classical antipsychotics and the newer atypical antipsychotics. They are also known as major tranquillisers. They are used in the management of major psychoses such as schizophrenia, psychotic depression, organic brain syndromes and mania. They all have an initial tranquillising effect and a more delayed antipsychotic action that reduces delusions and hallucinations. All have potentially serious side effects that will be experienced to different degrees by different individuals. As with antidepressants their use should be tailored to the individual person. In general, a psychiatric specialist initiates their use, and they are available as oral treatment and injections (both short-acting and long-acting 'depot' forms). Treatment may last for many years so it is important to get the right drug for the individual.

Classical antipsychotics

Table 20.6 Classical antipsychotics: common drugs used

Drug	Brand name	Dose range and route of administration
chlorpromazine	Largactil	50–1000mg oral and short-acting injection
sulpiride	Sulpitil	200–2400mg oral
flupenthixol	Depixol	6–400mg oral or depot injection
trifluoperazine	Stelazine	2–30mg oral
haloperidol	Serenace/Haldol	1–300mg oral and injection (both short and depot)
zuclopenthixol	Clopixol	20–23mg oral or 100–600mg depot injection

Common side effects:

- Sedation
- Dry mouth
- Increased appetite
- Weight gain
- Impotence
- Movement disorders (known as extrapyramidal effects).

Atypical antipsychotics

Table 20.7 Atypical antipsychotics: more common drugs

Drug	Brand name	Dose range and route of administration
clozapine	Clozaril	200–450mg oral
olanzapine	Zyprexa	5–20mg oral
risperidone	Risperdal	0.5–50mg oral and depot injection
quetiapine	Seroquel	300–750mg oral

Common side effects:

- Sedation
- Increased heart rate
- Weight gain
- Diabetes
- Excessive salivation
- Impaired reaction time
- Dizziness.

Psychological therapies

The talking therapies have been around for thousands of years, often supplied by the religious agencies, although as western society becomes more secular, trained professionals now more commonly offer them.

Talking therapies or talking treatments can be offered by a wide range of professionals such as psychiatrists, psychotherapists, psychoanalysts, counsellors, family therapists, clinical psychologists, specialist mental health nurses and others. Most patients receiving treatment from any of these professionals would not notice that much difference between them in what actually happens in the time spent together. The differences are more about type of training, choice of licensing or regulation and the practicalities of where and how the treatment is offered. The choice of type of treatment will more commonly be decided by what is available either through the health care provider or privately.

Rather than attempt to differentiate between the different types of talking therapy based on who offers it, a more useful focus is on the commonalities offered by all and some of the specific differences between the main paradigms; the theories and models that underlie the treatment offered.

There are two elements to the therapeutic relationship: the contractual professional service and the personal relationship or bond that develops between the therapist and client. Despite the fact that there are numerous types of therapy available and the practitioners may argue fiercely about the merits of one type of therapy over another, all have three basic factors. These are based around support, learning and action.

Support factors consist of:
- Reduction of anxiety
- Trust
- Reassurance
- Empathy
- Acceptance.

Learning factors consist of:
- Advice
- Feedback
- Insight
- Coming to terms with problematic experiences.

Action factors consist of:

- Testing solutions from the safety of the therapeutic relationship

- Facing fears
- Working through the problems
- Mastering the problems.

Most psychotherapy can be grouped into four categories:

- Cognitive behaviour therapy
- Psychodynamic therapies
- Person-centred or client-centred therapies
- Systemic therapies.

Cognitive behaviour therapy

Cognitive behaviour therapy aims to identify maladaptive actions or thoughts and correct the problem within a therapeutic relationship. In simple terms, what has happened cannot be changed but the individual's reaction to future situations can be modified to make life better. You do not have to keep making the same mistakes because of a learned pattern of behaviour following a stress. This is very much problem-orientated therapy and the client will be set homework tasks. The aim is to work in an open relationship to define and resolve problems. In mild to moderate depression it is as helpful as medication, but requires a much bigger commitment of time both from the client and the therapist. The therapy is usually fairly brief in nature, lasting in general about 12–20 sessions.

Psychodynamic therapies

Psychodynamic therapies focus on the correction of ingrained and insecure patterns of attachment and relationships. They stem from the work of Freud and are often prolonged, sometimes running into several years of therapy. They typically involve in-depth analysis of the client's life and rely heavily on the concept of transference to understand the client's problems with relationships. Transference is the projection of feelings and assumptions derived from an early relationship onto others. The feelings are experienced as real and the individual has no insight into their source. In simple terms, the dislike of a colleague for no apparent reason may stem from their resemblance to a person who abused them in childhood for example. The therapist will then use interpretation to link conscious and unconscious experiences. The interpretation is a tentative hypothesis for the client to consider and explore.

Person-centred or client-centred therapies

Person-centred or client-centred therapies aim to restore wellbeing through the self-expression of distress. A supportive and safe framework is provided for the individual to identify and find solutions to problems. This can take the form of supportive psychotherapy when the interview is itself therapeutic and includes reassurance, explanation, guidance and suggestion. In general it is non-directive, allowing the client to identify and resolve their problems within a safe therapeutic relationship.

Systemic therapies

Systemic therapies include group and family therapy and are the basis of therapeutic communities. They are based on the premise that the 'system' creates an individual's problem and work to change the system. Groups enable people to share experiences and gather information and resources in a safe environment. They develop socialising techniques and allow interpersonal learning. Groups can be educational, allowing a facilitator to impart information and the members to discuss it. These are usually closed groups with a fixed membership and of short duration. A typical example might be group work for people newly diagnosed with diabetes mellitus. Therapeutic groups are generally more flexible, often allowing new members to join and saying goodbye to old members along the way. This is known as an open group. A typical example of this would be the groups run by addiction treatment centres. Family therapy developed in the 1950s and is used widely by child and adolescent psychiatrists. The family is viewed as the system and an individual's behaviour as a reaction to the system.

With psychological therapies the relationship with the

therapist is paramount and far outweighs any perceived benefits between the different therapies on offer. Also of importance is the time commitment involved; the person needs to be clear as to what they are letting themselves in for. Finally, the person needs to be clear what their aims are and this must be honest and open. Entering any therapy under pressure from others is not likely to be successful unless the individual themselves has a clear aim and agenda.

Summary

Because of the nature of pharmacological regulation and the enormous sums of money to be made by the pharmaceutical industry there is a great deal of good quality evidence supporting the use of all drugs. However, there are relatively few trials that have investigated the benefits of psychological interventions, the talking therapies. Those that have been done tend to have concentrated on cognitive behaviour therapy and have shown considerable benefit from their use.

The recognition and treatment of psychiatric disorder can be a minefield. For the coach it is important to recognise that whilst the mental ill-health of the client may interfere with the relationship, so might its treatment. Both mental illness and their drug treatments can impair physical and psychological function. Even psychological therapies can impair functioning whilst the client deals with painful issues.

References

American Psychiatric Association (eds) (1994) *Diagnostic and Statistical Manual of Mental Disorders – Fourth Edition*, (DSM-IV) Washington, DC: American Psychiatric Association.

AC (Association for Coaching) (2005) 'Code of Ethics and Good Practice', 1 September. Available online at http://www.associationforcoaching.com/about/about02.htm (accessed 27 April 2006).

Bachkirova, T. and Cox, E. (2004) 'A bridge over troubled water: bringing together coaching and counselling', *The International Journal of Mentoring and Coaching*, 2(1) July. Available online at http://www.emccouncil.org/uk/journal.htm (accessed 27 April 2006).

Berglas, S. (2002) 'The very real dangers of executive coaching', *Harvard Business Review*, 80(6): 86–92.

Board, J.B. And Fritzon, K. (2005) 'Disordered personalities at work', *Psychology, Crime & Law*, 11(1): 17–32.

Casement, P. (1995) 'On Learning from the Patient', London: Routledge.

ECI (European Coaching Institute) (2005) 'Statement of Standards and Ethics'. Available online at http://www.europeancoaching institute.org/about_eci/standards_and_ethics.php (accessed 27 April 2006).

Gelder, M., Lopez-Ibor, J., Andreason, N. (eds) (2003) *New Oxford Textbook of Psychiatry*, New York: Oxford University Press.

Glasser, W. (1976) *Positive Addiction*, New York: Harper & Row.

IAC (International Association of Coaches) (2003) 'Ethical Principles and Code of Ethics'. Available online at http://www.certifiedcoach.org/ethics.html (accessed 27 April 2006).

ICF (International Coach Federation) (2005) 'The ICF Code of Ethics', 22 January. Available online at http://www.coachfederation.org (accessed 27 April 2006).

Jarvis, J. (2004) *Coaching and Buying Coaching Services: A Guide,*

London: Chartered Institute of Personnel and Development. Available online at: http://www.cipd.co.uk/guides (accessed 27 April 2006).

Lubit, R. (2004) *Coping with Toxic Managers, Subordinates and other Difficult People*, New Jersey: Financial Times Prentice Hall.

Martinez, A. (2004) 'Coaching: Is this Considered the Practice of Psychotherapy?', State of Colorado: Mental Health Trends. Available online at http://www.dora.state.co.us/mental-health/trends.htm (accessed 27 April 2006).

Szegedi, A., Kohnen, R., Dienel, A. and Kieser, M. (2005) 'Acute treatment of moderate to severe depression with hypericum extract WS 5570 (St John's wort): randomised controlled double blind non-inferiority trial versus paroxetine', *British Medical Journal*, 330: 503–506.

Williams, P. (2003) 'The potential perils of personal issues in coaching: the continuing debate: therapy or coaching? What every coach must know!' *International Journal of Coaching in Organizations*, 2(2): 21–30.

WHO (World Health Organization) (eds) (1994) *International Statistical Classification of Diseases and Related Health Problems, Tenth Revision*, (ICD-10), 2nd edn. Geneva: World Health Organization. Also available online at http://www.who.int/classifications/icd/en (accessed 27 April 2006).

WHO Collaborating Centre for Research and Training for Mental Health (eds) (2000) *WHO Guide to Mental Health in Primary Care*, London: Royal Society of Medicine Press.

Index